A MOTHER FOR ALL SEASONS

A Mother for All Seasons

~~~~~

DEBBIE PHELPS

with MIM EICHLER RIVAS

WILLIAM MORROW

An Imprint of HarperCollins*Publishers*

A MOTHER FOR ALL SEASONS. Copyright © 2009 by Deborah Phelps. All rights reserved. Printed in the United States of America. No part of this book may be used or reproduced in any manner whatsoever without written permission except in the case of brief quotations embodied in critical articles and reviews. For information address HarperCollins Publishers, 10 East 53rd Street, New York, NY 10022.

HarperCollins books may be purchased for educational, business, or sales promotional use. For information please write: Special Markets Department, HarperCollins Publishers, 10 East 53rd Street, New York, NY 10022.

FIRST EDITION

Designed by Laura Kaeppel

Library of Congress Cataloging-in-Publication Data has been applied for.

ISBN 978-0-06-178001-1

09   10   11   12   13   WBC/RRD   10   9   8   7   6   5   4   3   2   1

In loving memory of Mom and Dad

To Donna, Amy, and B.J., with gratitude

*To everyone who has played a role in the journey
I'm so blessed to be on*

*And, most of all, to Hilary, Whitney, and Michael, and to Taylor
and Conner, who have given me more joy and pride than can be
captured in words. I love you!*

CONTENTS

A MOTHER FOR ALL SEASONS

Team Phelps

With all the various hats I wear—as a woman and mother, as an educator for more than three decades, now as a middle school principal, and as a lifelong learner—I've never felt there was anything wrong with letting my emotions show when the situation calls for it. And that's just as well too, because I don't think there's much I could do to hold back my tears whenever I'm genuinely moved, humbled, proud, or inspired—although I do seem to become a waterfall at the most inopportune occasions! These instances happen with such frequency that behind the scenes in our family and among fellow members of Team Phelps they're affectionately referred to as "DP moments."

I'm pretty sure my amazing children—Hilary, Whitney, and Michael—all started calling them "Mom moments" early on, as in, "Oh, no, Mom's got that look, here she goes, get out the Kleenex!" The name was diplomatically converted to "Debbie Phelps (DP) moments" probably by Peter Carlisle of Octagon—not only one of the most brilliant sports agents in the business but also someone who is very sensitive in his own even-keeled way. Or my waterworks may have been rebranded by none other than Bob Bowman—one of the winningest swim coaches of all time—who plays a few roles on Team Phelps, including mentor and training strategist extraordinaire. Michael just calls him the "mad scientist."

Of course, it doesn't really matter who came up with the term, because I've certainly been blessed with a great abundance of DP moments—as I hope all of us have. And I loved every one of them! What matters, I believe, is that we don't take them for granted or let them pass by without stopping to embrace and celebrate them— whether it's with cheers, tears, homemade decorations, and elaborate festivities, or simply with silent appreciation.

I'm not just talking about the unbelievable peak moments when diplomas are received, when wedding vows are exchanged, when gold medals are won, or when new life is brought into the world. I'm really talking about breakthroughs of all kinds, like those smaller, less publicized moments when limits have been pushed and life lessons have been learned. And for breakthroughs to be possible, we sometimes have to embrace setbacks, those times when we (or our loved ones or our teammates) fall short of our goals or encounter obstacles. After all, if we don't acknowledge the disappointments and the tough times too, I don't think we can ever fully enjoy the triumphs.

It's also been my experience that the most memorable two-Kleenex-box moments are the ones that you can share with others—and that involve the whole team.

One that's right up there in the top ten DP moments for me took place in Athens, Greece, at the 2004 Olympics. This is a memory I've recalled in many settings, but with every retelling, I am filled with the same emotion and awe as I felt when I watched my then-nineteen-year-old son, Michael Fred Phelps, take his place on the blocks to compete for his first possible gold medal in the 400 meter individual medley (400 IM).

I probably hadn't exhaled from the instant when I'd first taken my seat in the stands with two of my three favorite people in the world, Hilary Kristin Phelps and Whitney Nikol Phelps. Glancing at Hilary to the right of me, I was reminded of the day when, at nine years old, she made a decision that would alter all of our lives. At the time, Hilary had begun the family tradition of swimming competitively. We'd started her at the Renaissance All-Sports Athletic Club (RASAC), which wasn't too far from where we lived in Harford County, about forty-five minutes outside Baltimore. Both Hilary and Whitney, who was seven years old then, were involved in lots of extracurricular activities, including the Brownies troop that I was proud to lead, as well as ballet and gymnastics. It never occurred to me back in those days that the girls—or for that matter Michael, who was still a toddler—would have such a natural affinity for the water. Not in the least. From the get-go, my water focus was all about safety and about exposing them to an activity that might spark their passion and interest. Little did I know where that would lead!

The first clue that Hilary was starting to take swimming seriously was when she announced that she wanted to become the next Janet Evans—the Olympic swimmer who had captured America's heart in that era. There was only one problem, as far as Hilary could see, and that was the place where she was training and the team she was on. She'd noticed that the swimmers who kept defeating her all happened to come from the same place—North Baltimore Aquatic Club (NBAC). Hilary didn't like being second or third, although she was satisfied as long as she was bettering her time—the name of the game. But she did enjoy the thrill of winning: being first. Instead of getting mad, she must have figured out the old adage "If you can't beat 'em, join 'em," or so I concluded when she announced to me, "I want to go to North Baltimore." Before I could debate, Hilary explained, "That's where the big girls swim fast and win!"

As fate would have it, when I went to talk to the coaches at NBAC, they had a spot for not one but two girls. Mind you, the distance from the county where we lived to the county where their aquatic centers were based was no hop, skip, and a jump—an expression I get from my mother and number one teacher in life, Leoma Davisson. In deciding how to juggle the demands of time and money on an already stretched budget and schedule, I always thought of my mother, who epitomized the idea that if something is important, you find a way to make it work.

Born and bred in a little town in rural, blue-collar western Maryland, my mother—an endless source of commonsense wisdom as well as quaint sayings—also knew a thing or two about having big dreams. Before she met my father, the aptly nicknamed Beau (for Bernard Joseph) Davisson, she was on her way toward a promising career as a concert pianist, with an opportunity to attend Peabody Music Conservatory in Baltimore. Though she sacrificed her dream to marry the love of her life and raise a family, I always believed she made that choice so that her children and grandchildren would be able to pursue their dreams to the hilt and take advantage of every opportunity life had to offer. So when Hilary set her heart on training among the best—to learn to swim fast and win—I knew I was going to move mountains to make that happen.

Sure enough, the change to the new swimming venue was worth it—in spite of the two hours on the road every night after school, regardless of carpools and other creative time-saving efforts. My credo, "Have minivan, will travel," kept me going even on weekends and evenings when I would have preferred being home, planning and writing lessons, grading papers, and taking care of all the other responsibilities that come with being a full-time middle school teacher. Meanwhile, before I knew it, both Hilary and Whitney were rising impressively in the ranks at one of the top aquatic centers in the state of Maryland, if not the country. Fortunately, by the time Michael was old enough to start swimming and competing, we had already moved to Baltimore County to be close to the multiple training facilities used by NBAC.

Maybe there was something prophetic for the whole family about Hilary's insisting that a move to a different club was important. In any event, looking back these many years later, I was and am convinced there are no real accidents in life and, indeed, everything happens for a reason. I also agree with Whitney, who once pointed out, "Some things *don't* happen for a reason."

So there we were in Athens, waiting for the start of the 400 meter IM as Michael finished his prerace stretching. Whitney leaned forward, taking it all in. Not as openly emotional as her sister perhaps, she was equally proud and intense about the race that was about to begin. She and Hilary each had their own histories of high expectations as competitors, but now their focus was on Michael. It had been Whitney who in her teens had qualified for the Olympic trials in 1996 and 2000; she had also set a standard of discipline and focus in the pool that raised the bar significantly for her brother. Did I wish I could have done something to help Whitney make it to these Games as a contender too? Absolutely. Then again, I knew nothing in the world could take away the joy that shone on her face the instant Michael dove from the starting blocks to take an early lead in the first fifty meters of the butterfly.

I didn't have a single moment of relaxation during this race—even after the split at the first wall put Michael a full body length ahead of the field. While he was favored to win, the 400 IM is a notoriously challenging event that demands ultimate precision and leaves no room for error. Nonetheless, as he kept up his pace, I did start to feel a little bit of joyful confidence surface above the other emotions competing for my attention. I knew Michael had two factors going for him—his uncanny ability to know his body's energy reserves, plus how and when to tap them to their utmost, and the fact that he had come armed with a game plan, a master vision for each and every event. And he'd rehearsed these in his mind and in the pool over and over, finessed to one hundredth of a second.

The one glimmer of concern, out of all four strokes to be swum in the 400 IM—fly, back, breast, and freestyle—was the breast-stroke. If any other swimmer out of the formidable field for this event could catch up with him, it would be in the hundred meters of the breaststroke. You never really can predict the outcome of what's often called a breaststroker's race.

Because of the clear delineation of roles on Team Phelps, I was fully aware that Michael and the relentless Bob Bowman had a strategy to counter any potential vulnerability. Whatever that was, I trusted their planning implicitly. And in my role as the mom on the team, my only job—as it had always been—was simply to be there with all my heart, all my being, and witness him come into his own, however that was going to play out.

Well, as basic as that sounds, when it came to making it to the Athens Games as a spectator and cheerleader, there were a couple of close calls that almost stood in my way. The first was a work-related conflict that came up when I had to choose between accepting the offer of my dream job—being made principal of my own school-house—or coming to the Olympics. There wasn't even a second's hesitation before I turned down the offer. True, I had spent close to thirty years in the Maryland public school system, as a teacher and an administrator with experience in a wide range of demographics, working toward just such an opportunity. But at every stage as I was ascending the ladder in my career, family still came first. That balancing act wasn't necessarily easy, however, particularly after my husband, Fred, and I divorced in the mid-1990s.

In time, I would come to appreciate the many lessons that I've been fortunate to learn as a single mom. But to deny the heartache along the way—for all of us—wouldn't be telling the full story I've chosen to tell. In fairness not just to myself but to everyone impacted on some level by divorce—adults and children—I have to note that most marital breakups are painful. Ours was no exception.

Although turning down the job didn't weigh on me in the least, I was very concerned about the failing health of my mother or, as she was lovingly called by her grandchildren, Gran, who at age eighty-five was battling an aggressive, rare type of cancer. Two years before, she had been told not to expect to live more than a few months to a year—a year and a half tops. As the second-born of her four children, I should have known she would defy those odds. Still, I couldn't avoid the thought of her being at a critical stage just as we were leaving for Greece. But no sooner did she settle into an assisted-living facility than her health and spirits rallied. Clearly, she was holding out for her dream to be realized—to live long enough to see her grandson swim in the 2004 Olympic Games.

Talk about setting a high goal! And as the overachiever that she was, she even went after it with style. With her energetic, vivacious personality, Leoma Davisson hadn't wasted a second in becoming the social butterfly of the whole facility. As we got closer to Athens, not only was Mom doing well, but she managed to gather together all her fellow seniors to watch Michael swim in the meets leading up to the games. She even attracted local and national media who wanted to get the story of Michael's grandmother and her Olympic highlights. If ever there was a member of Team Phelps cheering the loudest for Michael from a distance, that had to be Gran.

And so there I was, in Athens, Greece, the home of the Olympics—where the games were born in ancient times—standing side by side with my daughters, with Peter Carlisle and Bob Bowman somewhere nearby among the twelve thousand fans who had risen to their feet, cheering thunderously as Michael indeed made history. Laszlo Cseh of Hungary took bronze and U.S. teammate Erik Vendt, in an outside smoke, won silver. Michael not only charged to victory with a final time of 4 minutes, 8.26 seconds to win his first Olympic gold medal but also broke the world record of 4 minutes, 8.41 seconds that he had set during the Olympic trials in Long Beach in July.

Over the course of the Athens Olympics and the games of 2008 in Beijing, China, there were to be more and more highs. But the ultimate DP moment that sums it all up for me was there in Athens. It came after the race was over and Michael had begun his post-event routine, which included being greeted by his appointed drug tester and escorted to the mixing zone for media interviews, then a warm-down swim, followed by the medal presentation, a ceremonial walk, the actual drug test (part of an antidoping campaign Michael has championed), and then more media.

During all that, because of the very tight security and Olympic protocol, Hilary, Whitney, and I hadn't gotten a chance to come together and embrace him—the family circle that was our personal protocol. But after the medal presentation, Michael walked toward the crowd and tossed the bouquet up into the stands to his sisters and me. In those seconds, we were able to exchange expressions of connection and pride. But no words had yet been spoken. Before we could actually talk, we had to wait for Michael to call Hilary's cell phone and tell us where to meet him.

Her phone rang repeatedly during that time with calls of congratulations coming in from around the world. Finally she answered and nodded, letting us know it was Michael. He told Hilary he wanted the family to meet him at the fence between the warm-down and the competition pools.

As we stood at the appointed location, looking through the holes in the fence, we watched Michael walking toward us, peanut butter and jelly sandwich in his right hand, Coach Bowman to his left, and his first gold medal hanging around his neck.

Bob later told me that during the warm-down swim, he looked over at Michael and saw something unforgettable. "Of everything that was still to come," Bob recalled, "the smile on Michael's face after the first medal has never been matched since. My first reaction was that nobody could be that happy. Michael was."

I saw the same smile Bob Bowman described. And in that setting, as the sun went down in the sky, as he walked across the pool deck toward us, it was like visualizing all his years of swimming going through my head, chapter by chapter as if I were reading a book. Not just any book but a dramatic saga that promised many sequels. I saw him first as that little fun-loving boy, the one who was teased because of his big ears and who a teacher or two had said "would have trouble learning," a boy who never let a diagnosis of ADHD keep him from proving the naysayers wrong. I saw him in the pool at ten, starting to make a bit of a splash as he sped through the water in various events, then at twelve with gigantic plans and dreams, and then at fifteen with a vision all his own, always pushing past barriers, always extending his reach. And here he was, having accomplished what he came to do—to win one gold.

How did he feel? That answer was in his words when he pushed the medal through the chain-link fence toward me.

"Mom," he said, as proud as I've ever seen anyone, "look what I did."

I held the medal in one hand, with Hilary and Whitney helping me, as Michael and his sisters shared in the moment too. We remained that way for as long as we could stand there, just like that, the four of us, and Bob Bowman beaming knowingly because he had seen this and more, long before any of us had. It happened, unusually, without attracting any photographers or autograph seekers. It was a private, cherished moment for each of us, one that is etched in my heart and on my sleeve forever. That's a DP moment.

Though I've since talked about it in the media—especially what it meant to me and how there is nothing more glorious than witnessing a fellow human being attain a dream and be able to say, "Look what I did"—much hasn't been told about the real journey required to achieve that shared moment. As everyone on Team Phelps will attest, it has been a wild, unpredictable ride, with dramatic ups and downs, heartbreaks, disappointments, recovery, reinvention, courage, and tenacity.

In deciding to tell my part of the story, my motivation is not to "tell all." Oh, my goodness, no. As you'll pick up, holding on to a sense of privacy has always been and always will be important to me. My own mother once lectured me for being too prim and proper. When my eighty-five-year-old mom said that I needed to work less and be more adventurous to have more of a romantic life, I turned enough shades of red that she called me "English," her euphemism for being too straitlaced!

Where I am without inhibition and am definitely adventurous is as a mother for all seasons, there to give unconditional love and support during periods of growth and during struggle, offering humor, hope, commonsense advice, and encouragement for all our children and for each other. As a citizen for all seasons—of the United States of America and the world—I'm also adventurous in daring to believe that an Olympic movement whose time has come can enrich the lives of children, youth, and adults around the globe. To talk about those subjects, among others, is one of the reasons I decided to undertake the challenge of looking back at the past as well as to the future.

But most of all, I made the decision to tell my story in order to share with you the discovery that I made only very recently, one that I hope can inspire and uplift you as much as it has me. It's the simple truth that though life doesn't always turn out the way that you planned, sometimes it can turn out even better.

ONE

Home

The arrival of my sister Amy, the third-born child in the lineage of four that made up the Davisson pecking order, was a most auspicious occasion. The year was 1958. I was seven years old at the time and my big sister, Donna, was fourteen years old. We never really knew why there had been a gap of seven years between Donna and me, and then another gap of seven years before Amy was born. My mother always told us it was because she wanted to savor the first seven years of each of our lives. Two years after Amy's birth my parents conceived a fourth child, allegedly by surprise. That was my brother, B.J.—also a Bernard Joseph like Dad—who was considered to be a change-of-life baby.

While having their kids so spread out kept my parents busy, it was a bonus plan for me. The idea that I could just adore my younger siblings and watch them grow from infancy to childhood, with me getting to help raise them too, was thrilling!

So on that day when news came from the hospital that Mother's baby had been delivered—whatever that meant—and Dad told us we could go meet our new sister, I could barely stand still. That was me—energetic, active, a tomboy, and Daddy's little girl from the word go.

"Stand still, Susie," Dad told me, using my nickname rather than the more proper Deborah Sue—or Debbie, as everybody else called me from as far back as I can remember. He began to fuss with my hair, puzzling over how to put it into a ponytail. As he set his strong jaw with determination to get the job done correctly, I detected the pleasant smell of tobacco from the pipe he smoked only in those strategic areas of the house where Mother allowed it. Back then I usually wore my long, naturally curly dark hair neatly pulled back in a ponytail—thanks to Mother's agile fingers that could brush it and remove tangled knots in no time.

Dad didn't have the same hairstyling ability or, for that matter, patience. He did his best and then gave up, reminding me and Donna that if we didn't get going, hospital visiting hours would be over and we'd miss our chance to see Mom and our new baby sister.

I guess my ponytail had gone askew by the time we got to the hospital, but I wouldn't have known it if the ladies who worked at the check-in desk hadn't asked, "Who did your hair?"

"Daddy," I said matter-of-factly.

Everyone laughed heartily, including my father. For my part, I was just being honest. But it was also my first taste of being the center of attention, and I must say it was a great feeling. It was almost as memorable as the first sight of baby Amy Jo, who couldn't have cared less about my hair. I absolutely adored her from the instant I saw her in my mother's arms. Needless to say, I felt that way all over again when B.J. came along to complete our happy family.

And truly, when I think back to all my years of childhood and adolescence, they are filled to the brim with just about nothing but happy memories. That was the world that first shaped me—in a time and place I can't help but miss at certain moments, every now and then. However, when I visit the small town of Westernport, Maryland—one hundred fifty miles southwest of Baltimore and a hop, skip, and jump from the West Virginia state line—I wonder if it's really the same place where I grew up.

Of course the street names are the same, and it still has its equal mix of industry and nature, with the steady stream of smoke rising from the Westvaco paper mill, alongside the natural beauty of the mountains and the rich foliage. But in many respects Westernport today is a dwindling spot on the map, like so many other small towns in the United States, places where time and interest seem to have passed by as if lost to a bygone era. Few of the younger people stay around anymore; instead they grow up, go off to college, marry, move away, and put down roots elsewhere. That was true for me and for my siblings after we graduated from high school, as it pretty much has been for the generations who followed us.

What hasn't changed about Westernport, however, is the kindness, the decency, and the warmth of the community that has remained and that shares the same spirit of home and family that's at the heart of the wonderful memories I cherish of where I come from. Indeed, the farther I've traveled, the more I've come to see how fortunate I was to grow up in the kind of supportive, friendly atmosphere that thrives in the Tri-Towns, as we called Westernport and Luke on the Maryland side of the state line, and Piedmont on the West Virginia side.

Interestingly, our region of Allegany County has a proud and patriotic past going back to the time of George Washington, who successfully led his troops against the British at Fort Cumberland, which later developed into the biggest city in the area. The "Fort" part was dropped as Cumberland grew into a major trading post. About twenty miles south was the area that became the Tri-Towns. In the late 1700s, after the American Revolution was won, war veterans and their families were given tracts of land along the Potomac River, where they could build homes, and farm and raise livestock. Apparently, the settlers who came to our part of the region didn't have an easy time of it; they called our town Hardscrabble, after the thorny soil that was so difficult to cultivate. But as soon as a few industrious citizens realized they'd landed smack-dab at the intersection of the Potomac and George's Creek—an ideal stop for the riverboat trade transporting coal and timber—they quickly claimed this spot as the last, westernmost access point to the Potomac. And that's how our forefathers and foremothers shed the unlucky identity of Hardscrabble and took on the new name of Westernport.

By the time I was born—on April 17, 1951, in Keyser, West Virginia (because that's where the nearest hospital was)—local industries of coal mining and manufacturing were going strong. Westernport was never a rich community, not by any stretch. But in those post–World War II/baby boom years—back in the days when the mills and factories were all humming, and work was plentiful at the coal mines and at Kelly-Springfield Tires down in Cumberland—the Tri-Town area was a bustling little working-class metropolis. We used to say that the odor coming out of the smokestacks from the paper mill was the smell of money that would be putting food on people's tables.

That was a good feeling to have, knowing that people were able to take care of themselves. Well, that could have been my incurable optimism going there, but when I was growing up, I thought that our normal family and the day-to-day workings of an up-and-coming small town made life about as charmed as it could get. For me, there was nothing better than growing up in a modest but safe and comfortable house on the corner at 407 Hammond Street, surrounded by friendly neighbors, and being the daughter of Beau and Leoma Davisson, sister to Donna Jean, Amy Jo, and B.J. (little Beau). Mom named me Deborah Sue after Debbie Reynolds (but made it Deborah from the Bible), and she named Donna after Donna Reed, another of her favorite movie stars. Amy Jo was Mom's way of paying homage to Louisa May Alcott's *Little Women*, a book she found inspiring and enchanting. And well, there was nothing new about naming a son for his father. Being a part of our family made me feel I lived in the greatest place in the world. It was everything I knew or could imagine. It was home.

At the center of this ideal upbringing—as I think of it—was the enduring love story between my parents, two of the most caring individuals you could ever meet. And if you had ever met them, it would have been easy to see why they fell for each other in the first place.

Leoma was of Scottish descent, a striking beauty with her dark, thick hair and bright, soulful eyes. She also had the most ladylike, poised way of carrying herself and speaking, almost as though she came from an upper-class, highly educated background. Mother was born in 1919 and was raised in the tiny town of Lonaconing—just "up the creek" from Westernport on the road to Cumberland—where she'd grown up with not much by way of creature comforts. Her family had made it through some bleak periods. My grandfather, Mom's dad, Pap, worked for many years at the local public elementary school, where his job was to feed coal into the furnace that heated the building. Though I knew she was raised in a frugal household, I still had to marvel at how resourceful my mother managed to be. When push came to shove, Mom knew how to get a hundred dollars out of a dime—or more, if the needs of her family were at stake.

Growing up with so little was probably another reason she placed such a premium on our getting an education in order to better ourselves in life. This was especially true as it came to appreciating and developing our God-given talents, as well as our special interests and passions. Remember, she had sacrificed her talent when she decided to marry Bernard Joseph Davisson and forgo her chance to study piano at the Peabody Institute, despite her notable musical gifts.

But Leoma was a woman who needed to be in love in order to be happy. So it was no surprise that Beau Davisson—athletic, hardworking, tall, dark, handsome with his chiseled features, a man's man who carried himself with distinction and pride—was able to "sweep her off her feet," as the saying goes.

Dad was of Irish background, and he'd grown up in the Tri-Towns, from hardworking stock just like Mother. Despite the fact that he came from modest means and hadn't pursued an education beyond high school, my father had an entrepreneurial streak and never held back either from hard work or from trying different ways to improve our situation. Early on he opened his own small business—a paint store—where Mom helped out before she became a full-time stay-at-home mother. My father learned so much from getting to know his customers that he eventually went into contracting and became a subcontractor for Sears, Roebuck in their flooring division.

There were only a few issues that caused any friction between my parents. Not that I ever heard an argument as such, but there were a few occasions when I suspect my father had stayed out too late, had had one beer too many, or had come home later than he should have after a pickup game of softball with his buddies. None of the specifics are clear but I do remember a Christmas when Dad surprised Mom with an unexpected gift—a new portable dishwasher. That didn't go over so well, but the next Christmas, he made up for it by plucking at Mom's heartstrings with a beautiful upright piano. Whatever the upset had been, it was quickly forgotten.

That is, until the Christmas when he and his buddy brought home a freshly cut tree that he couldn't get to stand up. Eventually he tied a string around it and nailed it to the wall. Boy, was Mom unhappy about that. But they found a way to laugh, made up, and moved on.

This problem-solving approach, especially in relationships, spoke to one of Leoma Davisson's core philosophies. She believed that the worst thing you could do was to sit on your emotions and stew over hurt feelings when disagreements cropped up with those you cared about most. Her attitude was that there was nothing wrong with having healthy arguments, as long as there was respect on both sides. But as she often stressed, life is too short to get hung up about petty stuff. This is a philosophy that I completely embrace. Today my three grown-up children and I end every conversation by telling each other, "I love you." And with our busy, action-packed schedules, I always add, "Safe travels."

After all, as my no-nonsense mother used to say to me, "Debbie, you should never put your head on your pillow when someone is mad. You never know if you are going to wake up the next day." In the years to come, we would understand the reality of that observation all too well.

The only other touchy area that arose between my parents was the difference in their religious backgrounds. While Dad's family was Catholic, Mom was a Methodist, and she was adamant that her children were going to be raised as she was. After some deliberation, since my father wasn't a devout Catholic, he agreed to Mother's edict that her four kids attend and become members of the local Methodist church, where she taught Sunday school, played piano, and directed the church choir. I don't believe Dad had a problem with this, but the issue led to some controversy later on and came up periodically in discussions.

In fact, I can distinctly recall Mom saying when we were young that according to the Catholic church we were destined to burn in hell because we were being raised Protestant. That terrified me and was something I could never get out of my head as I walked to school and passed by Saint Peter's, the imposing, ornate Catholic church and school that stood in stark contrast to the smaller, more contemporary Methodist church where we were members.

I must confess in those days that I was afraid of the nuns who wore the full traditional habits—the long black gowns with the white head coverings and pointy hats. We had all heard what disciplinarians the nuns were supposed to be, using their rulers to hit the knuckles of the children who misbehaved. In my imagination, I could see them scowling and pointing before they would come and attack me like a swarm of birds and then send me to hell to burn.

I had that same eerie feeling whenever I walked down Philos Avenue, where the Catholic cemetery was on one side and the general community cemetery was on the other. I would hurry along nervously, fearful that the angry spirits buried in the Catholic graveyard would recognize me as a sinner and would come for me before my time. Of course, this just showed what a vivid imagination I had. When I grew up and actually met nuns who had made the choice to devote themselves totally to their religious beliefs and to a life of service—as teachers, in clinics and hospitals, and in work with the poor and needy—I developed a lasting respect for them. I think this process of discovering for myself that these nuns were not scary but actually people to be admired and respected also opened my eyes to how ridiculous and tragic it is when people discriminate against each other because of religious differences.

Perhaps it was this process—along with growing up in the loving Davisson family—that explains the open-minded side of me.

Just the idea that people can't get along because of differences in religion, race, class, socioeconomic background, or nationality is plain nonsense.

Some of the most pressing challenges I would face in the future as a public school teacher and administrator were the assumptions some people make about which children are capable of learning (or not), assumptions based on these very differences. More nonsense! I see children as children. No matter where they were born or how they live, each and every child is endowed with the same potential for learning and achieving. I am always inspired by the words of Baltimore County superintendent Dr. Joe A. Hairston, who often reminds us, "Our children are our future. We must teach them well. They deserve the best." To that I have added, "Every child is our child. We hold their heart in our hands each and every day."

Many of my early memories take me back to my home away from home at Westernport Elementary. I loved school! It was a very invigorating place for me. I loved my first-grade teacher, Mrs. Footen, an experienced educator who knew just how to motivate students. What made her classroom so special was the wonderful play corner she set up with games, toys, and a dollhouse I remember most of all. It turned out that her husband taught shop (industrial arts) at the high school; he had made the amazing dollhouse expressly for her students. After all the hours spent playing in Mrs. Footen's dollhouse, I emerged with a lasting interest in home economics—not to mention the dreams of having a home and family of my own one day.

While Mrs. Footen was older, more motherly and experienced, my next favorite teacher, Miss Winter, whom I had in second grade, was younger—a beautiful lady who taught me poetry and cultivated the love of books in all of us through reading circles. I can still see the proud look on her face as each of us took our turn to read aloud or when we showed improvement.

Like so much of my childhood, the years of my schooling were mostly joyful. That is, except for an incident in the fifth grade with my least favorite teacher, Miss Coughlin. She was a busybody, old and not much fun at all, and thanks to her severe clothing and heavy black orthopedic shoes, everything about her was austere. Instead of a desk with drawers, for example, she used only a plain wooden table, as if anything else would be too frivolous. But the main reason she stands out as one of my least favorite teachers was a great injustice that took place when it came time to cast the lead role in a play version of *Pocahontas*. I not only wanted the part but felt certain I was the best choice for the role. The other girl in contention wasn't tall and slender, as I was. Nor was she darker-skinned with captivating features and long, dark hair—all of which could be said about me. My hair could easily be braided as Indians wore their hair in the time of Pocahontas, whereas she would have to wear a wig. As logical as this was to me, Miss Coughlin went right ahead and gave the part to the other girl.

Later I did wonder if there might have been a lesson that I missed—as in, perhaps she practiced her lines more diligently than I did or came more prepared for the tryout. But at the time, I thought it was horribly unfair. Certainly I didn't dwell on it, although that was the first time I saw that life wasn't always fair. As future events would reinforce for me, who wins and who loses often comes down to a variety of factors, including the luck of the draw. Whether I liked it or not, sometimes an outcome wasn't in my hands but simply in the cards.

That said, the fact that not getting the role of Pocahontas in the fifth grade was the lowest point in my school life only underscores how positive the rest of my schooling was. A love for school was something that I shared with each of my siblings, no doubt in part because the value of education was taught us at home. The tradition started with my sister Donna, who would be our trailblazer as the first member of the family to go to college (Frostburg State, later renamed Frostburg University) and the first to become a teacher. In primary and secondary school, Donna was a serious student and known for her kind, nurturing demeanor. From early on, she had strong religious beliefs and always had a special place in her heart for adults and children who had different challenges.

Compared to Donna, I was more of an extrovert at school— high-spirited, fun-loving, but still always achievement-oriented academically, not to mention competitive in athletics and other extracurricular activities. Amy was outgoing in her own way; particularly, her creative drive led her to performances in various high school musicals. Amy was also an envelope pusher, where I was more of a Goody Two-shoes, not wanting to do anything wrong. Not my younger sister. Actually, Amy was the only one of us who could make my mother curse! But she too was college-bound and went on to attend Salisbury University and later pursued a successful career in human resources.

B.J. was as a child the closest to me in personality—a go-getter who excelled at whatever motivated him. Instead of an interest in sports—Dad's passion—B.J. inherited musical gifts from Mom, in addition to a razor-sharp intellect. After graduating from college, he ascended to the top levels of academic administration. Today he is vice president of university advancement at Frostburg State University (his alma mater), not too far from where we grew up in Maryland.

Even with the nine years separating me and B.J., we were the two peas in a pod, while Donna and Amy had a lot more in common with each other and were close, in spite of the fourteen-year difference in their ages. At the same time, we got along as a foursome, rarely encountering much if any of the sibling rivalries that can be so common. Maybe that was because Mom and Dad gave each of us ample attention and praise, along with enough structure to keep us busy and out of trouble.

Westernport may not have been the most exciting hot spot in the world, but I don't remember ever being bored. On the contrary, there were day-to-day adventures that I recall loving dearly—even just walking down the main thoroughfare in town, where we could see familiar faces and landmarks like Kenny's market, the library, the local police department, the drugstore where we could buy fountain drinks, Newcomb's pool hall on the corner, and the hot dog stand where they put Coney Island hot dogs to shame. Family field trips to Cumberland for certain shopping needs were welcome changes to the routine; we'd go down the road there to buy clothes at places like Sears and the Fashion Bug.

Every year at the end of summer, I looked forward to shopping for school clothes. If a special event came up during the year, we'd either shop for it at the time or, more often than not, take turns at the sewing machine. Later, during my high school years, Donna made my first prom dress. It was a pink dotted swiss (a lovely fabric) with embossed rosebuds—a scoop-necked, straight, full-length gown with puffy sleeves, with which I wore long white gloves and my hair up and shoes perfectly dyed in just the right pink. For the next prom, I would make my own dress. White with green-flocked flowers, it was strapless with a bolero jacket that I made out of curtains!

Many of my fondest memories of home are connected with the seasons. Every fall seemed to be more beautiful than the one before it—with the leaves in all the shades of brown, orange, yellow, gold, and red, as if the trees were putting on their prom dresses in their best colors to stage a show before winter arrived. Fall in the mountains of western Maryland was truly nature's masterpiece. This time of year also summoned the pleasure of great expectations—the new school year, your class schedule, and everything associated with the football season.

Even before I went to junior high and high school and became a cheerleader, football was already a way of life. In the Tri-Town area, as in many smaller and larger cities in those days, football was a huge deal, and all ages turned out for the games—not just to cheer for the home team but to socialize and get caught up on all the town gossip and goings-on. Football was even more meaningful to me because it was Dad's passion. And whenever football came on TV, he and I would be right there watching it together. He was an astute student of football too and taught me many of the subtleties that even the most hard-core fans might miss. Since I was the child most interested in sports in our household, that became something the two of us shared as father and daughter. On one very special occasion when I was about twelve years old, he and I rode in his van to Philadelphia to watch an Army-Navy game. What a rivalry! To be in a massive stadium like that and to hear the roar of the crowds from fans of both teams was a dream come true, at least for me at that age. I couldn't imagine anything better. Only time would lift that bar!

When winter rolled into Westernport, it brought with it another kind of beauty—a snow-covered landscape dotted by footprints and tracks as all the children tromped off to school, which was almost never canceled. And then there were the frozen nights with the clearest skies on God's earth, just sparkling with stars. When you almost couldn't take another day of winter, the relief and renewal of spring arrived. Spring was always as spectacular as you might suspect, given the above-average amount of precipitation that typically fell in the region. There was such an abundance of beautiful trees and flowers that I was always sure nowhere else in the world could have as many.

And then, of course, came summer, most of which we spent at the farthest tip of our state at Deep Creek Lake, about forty-five minutes from home. We had property there that we owned jointly with one of Dad's friends who was a lawyer. Each of our families had mobile homes that we kept on the property year-round. The summer days were filled with swimming, fishing, and water-skiing. Dad taught me to water-ski and I loved every second, skimming the glassy water, cutting back and forth over the wake on a slalom ski, sometimes with him skiing next to me, as I would duck under his towline, laughing and enjoying just being Daddy's little girl—as I thought of myself at every age.

And without a doubt nothing tastes better than food cooked outdoors, or so it seemed after many hours out on the lake, when the smell of whatever Mom was fixing up on the grill was the next best thing to the actual taste of it.

No matter what the season, my mother loved to celebrate the holidays and every other special occasion. Every Sunday, with few interruptions, we made the trip after church to drive up and visit her parents, Felix and Agnes Foote, or Pap and Gran as we called my grandparents. There were many rewards to come from watching Pap tend to his garden, where a variety of plants and vegetables flourished under his care, and then partaking of the treats that came out of my grandparents' kitchen. Gran concocted the world's most delicious root beer and Pap was known for his homemade saltwater taffy. My mouth waters just thinking about it, even to this day!

Our weekly trips to see our grandparents were never presented as a chore or an obligation, even though I know there were times when Mom had other matters she could have been home looking after. Family came first.

All these traits that I saw in my mother became values she passed down to me, less by what she said than by what she did. Though I was crazy about my father and certainly inherited much of his drive to succeed and his refusal to settle for mediocrity—something that I've never had much tolerance for—Mother set very high standards too. Whenever I have an opportunity to remind my students to value their moms and not to say disparaging words about anyone else's mother either, I share the story of my childhood and how Mom started me very young by teaching the importance of being a lady. Not in any phony or frilly fashion, but with character and stature. She demonstrated how to be poised, how to carry oneself with confidence and dignity, how to walk into a room and command respect without saying a word. And the other thing I learned from her was how to listen. Leoma was a keen, active listener. She could solve the world's problems, just by listening.

There were many other things I learned from my mother early on and later. But the one thing that just didn't take was how to cook. This may surprise you, coming from a home economics major and teacher, and from the mother of Olympic athlete Michael Phelps, who has talked extensively about his favorite things to eat. I wish the passion for cooking had come more naturally or that I had spent more time writing down some of Mother's homemade one-of-a-kind recipes for treats she used to make that we all remember fondly. Of particular interest has been an effort to replicate her recipe for no-bake cookies that Hilary and Whitney think they're closing in on with something along the lines of the following:

---

2 cups sugar, 4 tablespoons cocoa, $1/2$ cup milk—mix and bring to a boil in a small saucepan. Let it bubble for one minute and remove from heat. Add a pinch of baking soda, then blend in $1/2$ cup peanut butter, 3 cups old-fashioned oatmeal, 1 tablespoon Karo syrup and a teaspoon of vanilla, until well mixed. Quickly drop by tablespoonfuls onto waxed paper and let cool. Enjoy!

Well, although I didn't get the cooking gene, I'm glad to say that I did inherit Mother's love for family celebrations and for attending to all the details that make them memorable—like the major production that went into Thanksgiving every year. All of our relatives and members of our extended family from miles around would travel to Westernport to our house, which overflowed with so many of us that when it came time to eat, we were spread across two rooms. The adults held court in the dining room while children sat at a table in the living room. Whenever one of the older siblings or cousins moved away from the area and there was an opening for one of the teens to move up to the adult table, it was a special rite of passage that was remarked upon by everyone.

These days B.J. hosts the annual Thanksgiving dinner and the same protocol is maintained. Even though my parents are no longer with us physically, their loving presence can still be strongly felt. No matter how much time passes, I continue to miss them as much as ever, while I am all the more grateful to have had the two of them as my mother and father.

As I began to figure out in my teens, life wasn't as perfect as I'd once thought. But having the foundation of home and family that I'd been given made it about as great as it gets—even in spite of the tougher days ahead.

TWO

~~~~~

Life Adjustments

Winter seemed to come early and all at once toward the end of football season during my first year in junior high, which was then the seventh grade. It was a week before the Thanksgiving break, just after lunch, on what I recall was a cold, dark, and gloomy Friday, when our English teacher, Mr. Carter, told the class he had very grave news to announce.

Mr. Carter was a skinny, nondescript younger teacher with a crew cut and thick black glasses, both in keeping with the style of the early 1960s, at least in the Tri-Towns. He taught with great knowledge of his subject matter. He wasn't as dazzling as Mr. McGettigan, the handsome blond seventh-grade algebra teacher; I sat right up front in his class. But Mr. Carter had expertise and an experienced manner about him that went beyond his years. I could tell by his tone this afternoon when he called us to attention that nothing in his teaching experience had prepared him for what he was about to say.

Maintaining composure and a steady voice, he told us, "Our president, John Fitzgerald Kennedy, was shot a short time ago in Dallas and has been pronounced dead."

All at once there were gasps and tears, along with cries and expressions of disbelief. For most of us—who were twelve and thirteen years old—this was the most shocking thing that had ever happened in our lives. For me, it was the first time that I'd ever felt that kind of jolt that shook up the way I looked at life. It didn't go along with how I saw the safe, happy storybook existence of life in Westernport. The world around us would never be the same either.

Mr. Carter made a remarkable choice that day. Rather than ignoring our fears and pretending everything was normal, or insisting we get back to work, he acknowledged our feelings and confusion, admitting he didn't know much yet about what exactly had happened and who was responsible for the assassination of President Kennedy. Instead of fueling panic, he stayed calm and kept us informed as he learned any new information that could shed light on the situation.

The memory of Mr. Carter's composure, keeping tabs on the news and walking us through everything he learned, would stay with me for years as a lesson on how to communicate with young people when crisis occurs. As a parent, teacher, and now principal,

I can recall occasions when the inclination might have been not to tell the children what was happening—just to soldier on, muscle through, and take care of it. Yet what I've found is that if you can keep children informed about what's being done and even offer them a positive role to play, it helps them process things much better, in the short and long term.

Recently, in fact, when a severe storm knocked out the electricity at my school, plunging the classrooms into darkness, leaving the hallways lit by emergency lighting but only dimly and for a limited time, composure came into play. I was able to use my cell phone to call the appropriate school district and security offices, as well as BG&E, while remaining calm and confident when I went on the intercom to keep the teachers and students in the loop. It was as basic as saying, "I just learned that the storm took out a transformer on Liberty Road, and as you can see, we don't have lights." Since the lunch shift was beginning, I dismissed classes one floor at a time and sent runners with flashlights to guide those students to their lockers if they needed to get their lunches and/or lunch money, and then to the cafetorium to eat. Everyone rose to the occasion and pitched in, making sure that no one tripped or had trouble getting to the cafetorium, where we successfully served milk and juice and cold-cut subs to each of the groups. By flashlight, no less.

Part of my composure came from collaborating with the staff in keeping everyone safe and secure, along with having a plan that was executed fully. At the end of the day, when the lights finally came back on, I breathed a sigh of relief. It was by no means the same kind of crisis we faced as a seventh-grade classroom in 1963 when President Kennedy was killed, but Mr. Carter's composure at that time stayed with me.

Even though life soon returned to normal after that dark time in our nation's history, it was in my early teen years that I started to feel a little less sheltered and to notice that everyone in the Tri-Towns didn't live a storybook existence. It began to be apparent that though we were working-class and doing fairly well, other families were teetering on the edge of poverty or worse, and there were folks who, for whatever reasons, had issues with cigarettes and alcohol or had trouble maintaining their jobs and a stable marriage. Of course, this was called reality. But it was disheartening to see the suffering and the discontent, particularly whenever I saw that children were hurting. In my way of thinking, something had to be done to fix the problems. I think this was the point in my early life when the seeds for being a focused problem solver were first planted. Later on, there would be more than a few people who would say, "Debbie, you can't solve all the problems of the world," and I would think, *Yes, true, but why not at least try?*

It was also in my early teens that I had my first brushes with the downside to a small-town mentality. For one thing, with everyone keeping tabs on one another, it was unnerving to see how quickly gossip could spread and how so much time was wasted following the latest local soap opera. And for another, I started to bristle at the small-mindedness of people who were quick to judge the dreams and expectations of others as well as of themselves. These circumstances fed my desire to do well, to attain a reputation that would make my parents and my siblings proud. Now I can see the less-than-desirable results of self-imposed pressure to excel at everything and not to allow failure or mistakes to occur. But knowing it even back then probably wouldn't have changed my thinking much. Just ask my siblings!

By the time I was at Bruce High School, besides being a cheerleader, I played basketball and volleyball and I high-jumped. I loved sports but didn't grow up in the era of Title IX; back then there was little opportunity for girls' performance in athletics. Academically, I was in the National Honor Society and would eventually graduate among the top ten students in my class. Yet I didn't hold back from having fun, especially with all the extracurricular activities—sports, cheerleading, student government, Future Teachers of America (FTA), and Future Homemakers of America (FHA), all the hours spent directing the *Archives* work (our annual yearbook), plus the get-togethers, slumber parties with girlfriends, and outings that punctuated our weekends and special occasions throughout the year.

Then there were the dances organized by Miss Puzzy, a wonderful woman in Westernport, who came up with the idea for a Teen Hall that she oversaw—for no other reason than that she believed if teenagers were offered healthy outlets for having a great time, they'd choose those activities over getting into trouble. Sure enough, we all flocked to her hall in droves and danced our butts off to the latest hits by everybody from the Beatles and the Beach Boys to all the Motown stars and Elvis Presley.

Then, during football season, every Friday night after the home game was over and we waved good-bye to our parents and younger siblings, a big group of us would head down to Main Street to

Greens Restaurant, our local hangout and soda fountain where the must-have delicacy was french fries and gravy that we'd wash down with vanilla Cokes. These were no ordinary fries and that was no run-of-the-mill gravy. In all my later years of studying and teaching home economics, for all my belief that food science shouldn't focus so much on how to make a perfect white sauce, Béarnaise, or béchamel, I never discovered the secret that Greens used for making their unforgettable gravy or their irresistible large, crisp french fries. Well, as my more health-minded daughters might say today, *Uh, Mom, maybe you had to be there.*

Part of the fun of going to Greens was taking the stroll together down the cow path, as we called the cement-paved trail (I don't know why) that ran down the hill from the school at the top, through the woods, winding down through the trees, and into town.

The Friday night lights from the football stadium still lingered behind us but weren't enough to light the way along the cow path. Mind you, it wasn't total darkness, but there were stops here and there where you could pause in semiseclusion and get a fast smooch from your boyfriend. It was wild and exciting, yet so safe and tame by today's standards. You never knew who you'd see on the cow path getting a smooch, but by the time you made it to the parking lot behind the funeral home, past the bank, and into Greens, there would be a few new couples who'd wind up being serious items, at least for that night.

Amid all the years of high school, both in the classroom and in my social and personal life, there weren't many disappointments or challenges that I can recall. But there was the time when Dad came home one day from work and discovered that I had a lot of boys in the yard with me and we were practicing high jump together as we took turns running and leaping over a bamboo pole that we'd found to use.

Dad was very upset, much to my chagrin. He snapped the bamboo pole across his knee, without uttering a syllable. Actions spoke louder than words. Whether it was that he didn't like his daughter hanging with a group of boys or that he didn't like his recently mowed lawn being used for high jump practice, I don't know. In any event, it never happened again.

And then there was the time that I was chosen Archives Queen, as selected by the faculty and staff of Bruce High School, rather than being crowned Homecoming Queen—the result of voting by the football team and coaching staff. I had lost to Beth Jackson. She was one of my closest friends and a fellow cheerleader, and she was also outgoing, as well as smart, considerate, and popular, and she was the class president. Whenever I went over to Beth's house in the tiny neighboring town of McCool, we were always treated to dinner at Hamburger Haven, a local business that her father either owned or had an interest in. Because it was also a bar, getting to have a bite to eat in there was always an eye-opening experience for me.

Though I was happy for Beth when she presided over her Homecoming court, I must admit I still had a tinge of disappointment. Of course the Archives Queen's court was larger, I reminded myself. But having the football team choose her did make the feat she had achieved more impressive, or so I believed.

Not too long ago, Beth's daughter wanted to lift her mother's spirits by rekindling an old friendship for her. She learned that my daughters and I were going to be the grand marshals of the Autumn

Glory Parade in Oakland, Maryland. Through the help of my brother, who now lives in Oakland, a meeting was arranged to surprise Beth. She was taken to a home (not knowing that it was B.J.'s house) under a fabricated reason, and at the prearranged moment, I appeared. We hadn't seen each other in more than twenty-five years, but from the instant we looked into each other's faces, it was like no time had elapsed. We picked up the conversation as if we were still back in high school. That beautiful moment epitomizes what true friendship is all about.

All these many years later, I joked, "You know, Beth, you were Homecoming Queen, but I should have been Homecoming Queen. I really didn't like that at all!"

"Yes, but you were Archives Queen."

"Yes, but I wanted to be the more popular one with the boys." I went on to say that her victory was probably on account of her expertise at cartwheels and the fact that I couldn't do them as well.

We laughed about how competitive I was back then—and continue to be in certain situations!

Actually, there were only two instances that I can remember being really upset in high school. The first was in the tenth grade when my history teacher, Mr. Bance, offered some unsolicited advice one day as I was leaving class. He said, "You know, Debbie, you're a good student, but I know that you'll end up being married right out of high school."

I stood there, stunned into silence. I must have muttered something to make the point that he was wrong, but I turned my head so fast to get out of there and not let him have the satisfaction of seeing how extremely upset I really was, that he probably didn't hear me.

He was wrong, absolutely. But hearing that comment may have fueled my fire to make sure that he wasn't right.

Of course even then, I had already begun a storybook romance with my high school sweetheart—one of the stars of the football team, the love of my life, the boy with the bluest, most beautiful eyes I could imagine—and I did hope he would ask me to marry him one day. His name was Fred Phelps—or, as his birth certificate had it, Michael Fred Phelps—and he was a year ahead of me in school. Popular, sought after by lots of girls his age and younger, he also had an intensity that he kept below the surface but that made him all the more attractive. When Fred was a boy, he lost his father to illness, and that left his mother to raise him and his older brother, Bill, on her own. As I got to know Fred, I realized that these difficulties had given him a maturity and an independence uncommon in other guys his age.

But that's not what got me, I confess. The truth? Fred was a heartthrob! He was handsome, tall and sinewy, funny and bright, and a competitor in every sense of the word, *and* he was a gentleman. What's more, the rest of my family was as crazy about him as I was. Especially my father. The two of them got on famously. It was the football thing that they bonded over. And I think that not having a father of his own anymore drew Fred even closer to Dad.

Fred attended the same church that our family did. When he was younger, in fact, Mom had taught him in Sunday school. She already had a positive impression of him that only improved the first time he walked me home from Youth Group after one Sunday night. He was wearing a trench coat over his white shirt, looking very sharp, and then he sat down on the floor with five-year-old B.J. and pushed a truck back and forth with him. This made an extra big hit with Mom.

From the moment we started dating, Fred was welcomed open-armed into our family, often joining us up at the lake in the summer and for all the other holidays and special occasions we celebrated. At home with our families and at school, we were more or less the "it" couple. By the time Fred was approaching graduation, toward the end of my junior year, speculation began about when the high school sweethearts were going to tie the knot, even though both families saw the importance of higher education and finishing college.

Since my dream at that time was to get married and have kids—preferably four of them—I didn't mind the hints that others were starting to drop. And being a natural planner, I also couldn't help painting visions about our future fantasy wedding that would, of course, be the social event of the season—maybe even of the decade for that matter. After all, if you're going to dream, why not dream big?

But Fred had his own dream, and it didn't involve getting married, at least not right away. Fred wanted to play college football and then make it to the pros. In addition, he knew that an education was important no matter what he ultimately pursued, and he didn't want to be tied down to the responsibilities of raising a family too soon. That made sense to me, as did my belief that I could share in his dream—in seeing him do well at something he was passionate about. It didn't occur to me there might be a career or passion that I could pursue that would be as all-encompassing as being a wife or mother. But to Fred's credit, he encouraged me to think about a college education. Toward the end of summer 1968, when he left West-ernport for Fairmont State University—about three hours east in Fairmont, West Virginia—I had begun to toy with the idea of fol-lowing him there.

While I hadn't made up my mind about whether that was what I really wanted or if I wanted it simply because that's what Fred was doing, a conversation that I had with a guidance counselor early in my senior year clarified the issue. Her comments were spoken in the same well-intentioned tone that Mr. Bance had used in the tenth grade when he told me that I would be married just after graduating from high school. In our meeting, the guidance coun-selor nodded in approval as she reviewed my grades. In those days our high school curriculum had some classes that were considered part of a "business track" while other classes were under the head-ing of a "college track." I had an excellent academic record—which happened to have been in a business rather than college track—so I was surprised when the guidance counselor told me, "Debbie, I think you would have no problem getting a job at the mill right out of high school."

I was definitely taken aback. Saying nothing, I waited as she explained that employment at the paper mill could lead to oppor-tunities for advancement. Or, she noted, "You could think about becoming a secretary. Your typing, shorthand, and bookkeeping skills will put you at an advantage."

Actually, in later years, my typing would be an asset to my work as a supervisor in the school system when many of my colleagues hadn't learned the fundamentals of keyboarding and still had to contend with two-finger hunting and pecking.

But once again I was crushed that someone in a position of authority in my high school could hold such a narrow view of my potential. "Well," I countered, "my sister Donna graduated from Frostburg State and is teaching already. I thought that might be a possibility for me." I had also been thinking how Mother had given up an opportunity to go to Peabody and how she wanted a college education for all her children.

"No," the counselor said, shaking her head, "I see you settling down, getting married, having babies. A job at the mill would be much more practical." Basically, she was telling me that not everyone was cut out for college.

If looks could have killed, who knows what might have happened before I calmly gathered myself up and left her office. All of a sudden, the mission to prove her wrong became more important than anything else. I was incensed. Who was she to doubt me? Needless to say, the word *no* had made everything perfectly clear. I made up my mind then and there to attend Fairmont State University and graduate from college before getting married.

In spite of that guidance counselor's negative message, I was fortunate to find others who saw my drive and were willing to encourage it and articulate their belief in me. One of those individuals was Mrs. Dye, my senior year English teacher, who was passionate about her subject matter and creative about planting seeds for our ongoing interest in reading and embracing learning of all kinds. I remember studying Shakespeare's *Macbeth* in her class and doing an assignment in which we were challenged to create a coloring book to get to know the characters and their speeches.

Before I had committed to a career path, Mrs. Dye was the role model who most closely epitomized the kind of teacher I wanted to become. The message that she sent to me was that I would be an excellent teacher if that turned out to be the direction I eventually chose.

Mr. Chaney, the assistant principal of Bruce High School, truly championed me, taking me under his wing, letting me know he had high hopes for my future. After assigning me to duties as his office assistant my senior year, he gave me an early preview of what a school administrator does—and also became a role model for how I might want to pursue such responsibilities later on. When it was announced that I had been selected as the only girl from the twelfth grade to attend Girls State, I knew that Mr. Chaney—a member of the American Legion, the organization that sponsored the conference each year—had played an important behind-the-scenes role in recommending me.

Attending Girls State, which was held at Goucher College in Towson, Maryland, a location that would one day be my stomping grounds, was life-changing. It was a crash course that not only gave me a taste of what university life was like but also provided lessons in leadership and competition. And I loved every minute of it.

The other opportunity I was given to travel in high school was to a Future Homemakers of America convention held in California. That was so exciting! The entire family came along to see me off at Dulles Airport as I met up with fellow future homemakers, all of us in fashionable late 1960s attire that many of us had designed and made for ourselves—with higher hemlines and matching hats! B.J., who was all of seven years old at the time, remembers what a big moment this was in the Davisson family history. He also recalls that this was in the days when, even as a child, you dressed in a coat and tie to go to the airport. He also reminds me now and then of how Mom and Dad cried when I walked out to the plane.

All these experiences shaped my interests in positive ways. A memorable influence from this time was Mrs. Schultz, the state officer for FHA, who left a lasting impression on me by embodying the best traits for both a supervisor and a home economics expert who worked outside the home. She was elegant and warm—someone who could take charge without being bossy. In short, Mrs. Schultz represented the ideal of feminine strength in her field that I wanted to emulate. Even though it was the late 1960s and there were drastic changes happening in popular culture and politics—including the protest of women's traditional roles as being unduly tied to the home and family—Mrs. Schultz didn't defend against criticisms that home economics might be seen as old-fashioned. To the contrary, she motivated us to consider ways to update our views and approaches to address those changes. I could see that she recognized my interest in such an undertaking.

With these empowering messages sent by Mrs. Dye, Mr. Chaney, and Mrs. Schultz about my potential, I knew that nothing could change my plans to attend Fairmont State.

Well, almost nothing.

The first wrench was thrown by Fred when, not long into his freshman year at Fairmont, he decided that we needed "space." Did I love the idea that he wanted to date other people? No. But since I had never really dated anyone seriously other than Fred, I decided to enjoy having space myself and go out with a guy named Danny Wade, who was also on the football and wrestling teams and was handsome too.

One Friday night at the football game, when I was standing on the sidelines in my cheerleading uniform during a break and was planning to go out on a date with Danny afterward, I turned around and there was Fred—who had decided to surprise me by coming home unannounced. I can still see him under the Friday night lights: bright-blue eyes, wide, confident grin, like he was Prince Charming holding my missing glass slipper and I was supposed to jump up and down and throw myself into his arms.

I didn't think so. Without beating around the bush, I let him know I had a date to go to Greens after the game with Danny Wade.

"What?" Fred asked, his whole face flushing red. Shocked and upset, he said little else but looked as if he'd been knocked to the ground.

"I didn't know you were coming home," I told him calmly. "You said you needed space and that we should date."

And that's what I did by keeping my date with Danny that night.

Not long after I returned home, there was a knock at the door. I went to it, and found Fred, who wanted to let me know that he felt strongly we had both gotten enough space after all and that we should get back together. As much as I liked Danny, I agreed. The bottom line was that I was in love with Fred Phelps and there wasn't much I could do about it. Not then and not later.

When I graduated from high school in spring 1969, I felt as if the world of exciting possibilities had opened like never before and things were just going to get even better. That same summer, I watched on television along with the rest of the world when the Apollo 11 mission made history by landing on the moon. Right in front of my eyes, I saw the flag of the United States planted on the moon and witnessed Neil Armstrong walk across its surface as he spoke his immortal words, "One small step for man, one giant leap for mankind."

What an incredible, inspiring time to be alive. All things truly were possible.

With that in mind, I embarked on the adventure of going to college—and accepted the challenge of how to pay my own way. In the process, I adapted my plans by deciding it would be better to stay closer to home by attending Allegany Community College in nearby Cumberland. This would allow me to save on room and board while going to school and working part-time. I couldn't explain why exactly, but I was suddenly not in such a hurry to be far from family. But maybe deep down, I had a premonition that it was important not to fly the nest all at once.

It wasn't long before that premonition made sense. The news landed like a bomb when we learned that Dad had been to see specialists at University Hospital in Baltimore City—and they had discovered that he had colon cancer. Immediately I said I was going to drop out of school to help Mother take care of him and drive him up to the doctors, stay with him at the hospital, whatever was required, but he wouldn't hear of it.

"Don't worry about me, Debbie," he insisted. "They have new treatments for this and I'm gonna be fine."

When Beau Davisson made a pronouncement like that, with

that level of authority, there was no doubting it. He was making a statement of fact.

Still, it was impossible not to worry about someone who had barely been sick a day in his life. The thought of ever losing him was unbearable. I worried about Amy and B.J., aged eleven and nine, and my mother too, who had never needed to go out in search of work because Dad was our rock of support. But following my mother's practical example, we all came together as a family to expect the best outcome. Donna was living and working in Harford County, but she took an active role, as did I, by making the trip as often as possible with Dad for his treatments when Mother couldn't go. Fred was also very supportive, always checking in when he could and getting Dad on the phone to talk sports and other subjects of mutual interest.

By early 1970 we started to see improvements, all of which were causes to be hopeful. Although Mom would never have let us see her fear even when it was there, she kept her spirits up throughout the year. Beau Davisson was the most optimistic of all of us.

After my classes had wrapped up at ACC for the first year, Dad sat me down and said, "I really appreciate that you've kept a close eye on me, Debbie. But the doctors are taking care of me and you don't need to worry anymore." His main point was that he wanted me to have the experience of going away to college and obtaining the quality education I could get at a four-year institution like Fairmont or any place of my choice.

In reality, I'd never taken college trips to visit different campuses; I wanted to follow the man I loved. My father knew that's what I really wanted to do. He also let me know how proud he was of me, a moment that I would cherish forever: it remains right up there in my top ten.

Fairmont State University was all that I'd been dreaming it would be and more. Well, I didn't make the cheerleading squad—on account of those pesky cartwheels and unladylike flips that I never liked to do. But I did join a sorority and found myself with a widening circle of supportive friends who were a lifeline to helping me obtain the on-campus jobs that I needed to pay for my education. Between social activities, work, and the classes, which I really loved, certain life adjustments to the storybook version of college had to be made. Still, all in all, I was grateful for everything—especially that my father was hanging in there.

Whenever we could, Fred and I made the trip home to keep close tabs on Dad's progress and just to spend time with him, along with the rest of both our families. The best opportunities for such visits came at the various school holidays, when classes weren't in session—such as the spring break that took place in April 1971. Though all my sorority sisters and Fred's fraternity brothers were headed south to Florida for days of partying and having fun, it honestly didn't cross my mind to go with them. I was eager to get home. Besides the fact that the break came the week before my birthday, which was coming up on April 17, and which we could celebrate belatedly with family, I was also looking forward to Easter and all the annual church and community festivities that went along with the holiday and the time of year.

But it was not a festive atmosphere that greeted me on the Thursday evening before Good Friday after we arrived back in Westernport. Fred noticed the serious mood too as he walked me into the house to greet everyone before going to his mother's house. The house was full, with Donna home for the Easter holiday, and Amy and B.J. there as well, but someone was missing.

Mom quietly explained that Dad was back in the hospital down in Cumberland, having taken a turn for the worse.

We'd been through these bumps in the road before, and since I believed it when he said the doctors were going to pull off a miracle, I wasn't going to allow myself to worry all over again. Then I thought to ask Mom, "Well, how soon will he be out?"

Instead of answering, she said, "Debbie, you should go see him now."

Not yet detecting the somberness of her tone, I shrugged and said, "I'll go see him tomorrow. He'll be more rested."

Mom, not morose or tearful, but with a resolute nod in my direction, then said, "You need to go see him *now.*"

That's all she needed to say for me to understand that my father was in serious condition. Still, I refused to accept that medical science and the brilliant minds of the world—who could pull off miracles like putting a man on the moon, after all—were giving up on saving my dad.

Fred and I immediately got in the car and drove to Cumberland.

When we arrived at the hospital, the nurse greeted me with relief, saying, "Oh, you must be Debbie," and acknowledged Fred. I didn't know what to say. As I walked into the hospital room, everything became a blur, and I felt so helpless. There was my father—thin and frail, looking much older than he should for a man who was fifty-one years old and who had hardly ever been ill. But still it was my dad, very much present, brightening as I walked into the room, with Fred trailing after me.

I held Dad's hand, and he asked me about my classes and said he was so glad to hear it was all going well. We just talked normally, and I was flooded by memories of growing up as the tomboy tag-along with her dad—the two of us watching football games together on TV, and me riding with him in his van, sitting up high, feeling so proud of being his daughter as we drove through town. And I thought of him in his true element: cheering and loving every minute of the hometown games out at the high school stadium under the Friday night lights. With so much life in him, nothing could have convinced me that he wouldn't rally and beat this. Miracles happen every day, I reminded myself.

When it was time to leave, I gave him a kiss and a hug, telling him I would come to see him every day that I was home. He didn't respond to that. Instead, he directed his remarks to Fred, saying, "I want to ask you to look after the family for me now. Take good care of my girls and B.J. too."

Doing his best not to break down, Fred promised that he would.

When we walked out of the hospital room, I was not ready to accept that I had just said good-bye to my father for the last time. But he did seem to be in a state of acceptance, even peace, with a slight smile on his face as he began to drift off to sleep right before we left.

In the middle of the night—the early hours of the next morning, on Good Friday—the hospital called to say that Dad had passed away in his sleep. Perhaps because my siblings had been to see him earlier and had been bracing for this event, they didn't seem to be in the same state of shock I was in. Mom, in fact, was prepared enough that she had made sure a priest was able to give Bernard Joseph Davisson his last rites. Because of the controversy over his being a lapsed Catholic—with a wife and children who were Protestant—the priest almost didn't administer the sacred last rites. But Leoma Davisson rose to the challenge, pled her case, and saw to it that Dad was given his last rites by a Catholic priest.

Throughout those next days before the funeral, and for a long time afterward, I couldn't bring myself to accept that a miracle hadn't spared him. I believed in and trusted the doctors, when the reality is they are only human. What did seem miraculous, if I allowed myself to acknowledge it, was how my father had mustered the strength and the will to wait for me to come home on break so he could see me one last time before he left us.

That had to be the cruelest spring I ever lived through. The ground that I walked on, the foundation, had been shaken forever. What made it ironic and even more painful was that the weather the week that Dad died was magnificent, everything in bloom, all the flowers and trees bursting with life, color, and vitality. In a season of new beginnings, incongruously, my father had died, in his prime, a week before my twentieth birthday. With Donna starting her teaching career, me still in college, my mother was left on her own to do what she could to be there for the two of us and to raise the younger two at home, Amy thirteen years old and B.J only eleven.

In later years, whenever anyone would ask how I found the ability to juggle some of the challenges I would face as a mom, I'd invariably say I'd learned from watching my mother respond to the blow of losing her husband and rise to face challenges she'd never known. Starting with next to nothing, she would eventually find her way into a longtime job as a teaching assistant—at which she was truly in her element. I know that if given the means or the time to have gone for her college degree and teaching certification, she would have thrived even more at that level. But Mom turned the job of teaching assistant into an art form that she mastered at a very high plane, with her pronounced love for children, her patience and passion for working with them, and her gifts for inspiring lifelong learners.

On not much more than three thousand dollars a year, she managed to keep it all together. It took her some time to find her footing, without question. But she did it with incredible grace under fire, never crying poor or sinking to self-pity or panic.

I should note for the record that because I was already out of the house and went right back to college after that Easter break, I didn't go through the same ordeal my younger siblings did. B.J., for instance, would later confide how heart-wrenching it was to hear our mother, alone in her room, crying herself to sleep at night.

At the funeral, which was early in the week after Dad passed, I remember how everyone kept telling B.J., just a young kid, the same thing. "You know," everybody said, in essence, "you're the man of the house now. You have to take care of your mother."

I know that many of the countless family and friends who filled Saint Peter's Catholic Church to pay their last respects were as much in a state of disbelief as we were. No one knew what to say except to express how sorry they were for our loss and to remind my little brother of his responsibilities as the man of the house.

Looking back, I've often thought that was too much to put on his young shoulders, although he learned to adapt to changes that affected us all.

Besides the onset of grief, there was a certain surreal quality to being inside the large, ornate Saint Peter's, with its marble floor, so different from the carpeted floor and contemporary sanctuary at our church. Walking in, Amy started to grow faint and Mom had to bring out the smelling salts.

During the funeral and the burial afterwards, my mother maintained her composure. We never saw her fall apart. I have no idea how she orchestrated all the particulars involved in putting together the funeral. I later learned that a loving individual paid for the headstone for my father's grave, making sure expense was not spared. It had been decided early on when Mom bought three plots in the public cemetery that Dad would be buried there, as opposed to the Catholic cemetery. In years to come, B.J. had the same eerie feeling walking past the two graveyards that I used to have when I was young, as if it were a problem with the spirits of the dearly departed that he was over on the other side.

After all those years that Dad hadn't been very observant, it was a miracle in itself that Leoma Davisson was able to have the service held at Saint Peter's—with our Methodist minister presiding, no less. Even though it was unconventional, she was determined to have a combination service that honored both sides of the family, Catholic and Protestant. Plus, she had her heart set on acknowledging our minister who had been so supportive to us over the years. And she pulled it off.

One of the ironies my brother remembers is how the funeral

home was filled with flowers, and how Mom thought it was so beautiful. In actuality, Dad hated flowers and would frequently grumble that too many arrangements made things look too much like a funeral home!

Even though I hadn't begun to measure how much my life would change with the death of my father, I knew that the world was never going to be the same place without him in it. Fred Phelps, who would a short time later announce that we should get pinned, the next step before getting engaged, was visibly shaken during the funeral proceedings. In light of subsequent events, I've wondered at times if the loss of my father had been more traumatic for him than he ever admitted. It was not only the loss of his future father-in-law but also the loss of a father figure who had helped to fill a void in his life. Unfortunately we didn't have the communication skills to ever talk about that or his feelings of loss.

At different stages in our future, I would find myself regretting that we hadn't talked more in depth about many subjects and wishing we could go back and air some of what had been left unsaid.

I wish I'd done lots of things differently. For instance, what if I had been more involved in the care and treatment of my father's illness? What if I had spent more time with Dad in those last years and could have told him everything I'd forgotten to say? There had been moments and opportunities I'd missed, when I should have done more, said more, sought more answers. Maybe nothing would have changed, but the more thoughts of "what if" and "could have" and "should have" and "if only" nagged at me, the more futile I realized they were. The life lesson that arose from this process came in the form of common sense (*C.S. thinking* being the operative phrase I emphasize daily), with the following note to self that I've tried to live by and teach:

Cherish your time and use it wisely. It's the one thing you can't get back or give back. No do-overs allowed. As it is said, life isn't a dress rehearsal.

Meanwhile, a tough two years of my life followed. The sadness that is conjured by memories from this period is not only for our family's loss but also for losses shared with me by friends and colleagues and for the unexpected curves that life throws us. I've also grappled with the saying that time heals all wounds. I sometimes wonder if that's really true.

Recently, I had the honor of meeting Lenny Moore, the football star and hero who was one of the first African Americans to play for the Baltimore Colts and who happened to attend an event where I was with Team Phelps amid an array of prominent sports figures. I approached him and introduced myself, saying, "You know, Mr. Moore, I watched you with my father when I was a little girl, and you brought so much happiness to him and so many fond memories to me now. Thank you." I told him we had lost my father much too young, many years ago, and that it had been a difficult time. But then again, I added, I knew how happy it would have made my father to know what special human beings his three grandchildren, my children, had become, not to mention how pleased he would have been to know that I'd met one of the greats of our home team—before the era of the Baltimore Ravens, that is.

Lenny Moore could see the emotion welling in my eyes, I'm sure. He smiled, took my hands in his, and asked what my father's name was. And I answered proudly, "Bernard Joseph Davisson. But his nickname was Beau."

~~~~~~

THREE

A New Season

Structure came to my rescue. For the next two years, though I had fallen from the giddy heights of happiness where all things were possible down to rock bottom where the worst had come to pass with the loss of my father, the power of putting one foot in front of the other got me through. Time worked for me as I tried to milk every second—keeping my focus on classes, homework, and my job scooping ice cream on the serving line in the campus café. I was very fortunate that Fred's fraternity advisers looked out for me as well and were able to recommend me for grants—everything and anything that looked remotely applicable—that allowed me to stay in school. No one ever made me feel like a charity case, but they knew I needed the money, so whatever they could find, they steered my way.

Majoring in home economics education was a natural fit, given my upbringing. By the time I graduated, though, I'd taken enough science classes that I might have gotten another major or taken another career path if I had chosen to. So much for the teacher and a certain guidance counselor who'd predicted I would marry right out of high school or that I wasn't cut out for college. While the dreams of getting married and starting a family were still at the top of my priorities, I was fortunate to have this time to weigh career options and all kinds of interests. Going from the small town to the bigger campus was also an important stepping-stone in between the sheltered Tri-Towns and the real world waiting for me down the road. Fairmont, West Virginia, wasn't New York City or even Baltimore, for that matter. But it was the right place at the right time that helped me grow and thrive.

The surrounding small towns like Mannington and Rivesville, where coal was mined and life was slow, seemed familiar to me. Campus life, however, clipped along at a busy pace and opened my mind to new ways of thinking. When I was rushed by my sorority, Phi Mu, I was excited at the mix of diverse backgrounds and cultural interests of my sisters, a group that included but was not limited to artists, musicians, actresses, athletes, and student leaders on our school campus.

At Fairmont, the Friday night lights still shone for me and Fred Phelps, who was playing football at a college level, even though the games were on Saturday afternoons. With his flair for fun and drama too, he added his own pizzazz to my social whirl. There were fraternity dances and trips to local taverns with jukeboxes blaring "Color My World" by Chicago and the latest hits by Elton John, and the parties with Fred's fraternity, Tau Kappa Epsilon, and everybody talking about a crazy punch they called Purple Jesus, so named for its color and the fact that it could knock you on your behind. Those high-spirited times all made for fond memories.

By the start of senior year, I was coming into my own and making a name for myself on campus. I was elected president of my sorority, and that gave me the chance to work in national philanthropy with Project Hope, whose mission was to take care of those less fortunate. At the same time, I did my student teaching, which was an amazing thrill. Fred took time off from school in order to work and put some money in the bank before coming back and completing his degree.

Meanwhile, I was having a taste of independence living off campus with three other girls. Perhaps because of the loss of my father and the difficult time that I'd gone through, my roommates and others began to turn to me as someone they could confide in and someone who could offer advice. If that was so, I was really only following my mother's example by being an active listener and by trying to give honest, thoughtful, commonsense feedback. In any event, the stories I heard from others were beyond my realm of experience. There were confidences from those who were dealing with pregnancies and decisions over whether to keep their babies or whether to choose to have an abortion. There were girls who were struggling with breakups, their boyfriend's infidelities, and something that at the time was highly controversial—interracial dating. There were girls who had self-esteem issues and were dealing with weight and image problems that led to bulimia and anorexia. Some of these stories were shocking, I have to confess, but in hindsight I'm grateful I had time to be exposed to issues that many girls and young women face.

As for the future, a lot was up in the air about where I was headed, but one question had been settled early on. This occurred during a visit home when Fred suggested that we drive to Cumberland and take a stroll in Constitution Park. We stopped to sit on a bench next to a fenced-off area that had deer roaming around inside it. It was like something out of a pastoral painting—a poem. Beautiful! And there in the park, in front of a deer looking on, Fred pulled out a ring and asked very simply, "Would you marry me?"

I cried, of course! And it was out of happiness, needless to say. And then I realized he was waiting for an answer. "Yes, absolutely," I answered. We embraced each other happily, as that deer is my witness.

We agreed to set the date for after graduation; it was eventually pinpointed as May 19, 1973. Fred returned to Fairmont to finish college while I rounded out my work experience credits by taking a job at an area hospital as a food supervisor. Talk about a rude awakening. If I had ever considered working in food service in a hospital, that job put a stop to that. For one thing, there was little I could do to improve the well-being of the sick people. For another, the setting reminded me too much of Dad during our last visit.

As I remember, there were five supervisors, and we rotated responsibilities for the writing of diets for patients, supervising the serving line, and taking care of the dining room that serviced the medical staff and visitors; together we did the inventory and ordering. The real saving grace and the only thing that made me happy at the hospital was getting to visit the nursery and seeing all the babies. No matter how dreary the rest of the hospital was, the moment I walked into the nursery and marveled at the new life being brought into the world, I was happy. I was naturally drawn to children and babies, and making these visits to the nursery added to the joyful expectation that came with being engaged and planning a storybook wedding that would soon be followed by the beginnings of a family.

It never dawned on me until later that throwing a wedding a week after graduation might be a bit, oh, perhaps, ambitious. Suffice it to say, the full plate of completing credits, studying for finals, working at my job, and preparing for graduation and a wedding the following week was a crash course in time management! And sleep deprivation. But I don't regret a single lost second of rest because I got to have the dream wedding I'd been planning in my fantasy for years. Fred acquiesced to every suggestion or request for approval with a "Yes, Debbie," or just a shrug of his shoulders. He was more than happy to let me take charge.

It was certainly the biggest wedding to hit the Tri-Towns probably ever, with hundreds of people in attendance and everything arranged down to the smallest details. There were eight bridesmaids, including my sister Amy and my friend Beth Jackson from high school, who had gone into nursing, plus a few cheerleading friends from ACC and some sorority sisters from Fairmont. My sister Donna served as my maid of honor. In celebration of the season, my bright color scheme was green, yellow, and orange, and we all carried parasols, which I had made from fabric to match the bridesmaids' dresses that I had whipped up too. While I've always resisted giving away my secret for those parasols, I'm now willing to pass it to you in the hopes that it may mean resurrecting a lovely wedding touch:

> Start with the frame of a child's cloth umbrella and remove each pane of fabric, replacing it with the fabric of your choice and securing each section with fabric tape. Wrap the handle in matching ribbon.

Making sure we didn't overdo the color, we had the groomsmen wear understated yet classic white tuxedos. At the last minute Fred realized he had forgotten his socks and ended up wearing a green pair—which, as our luck would have it, matched!

I have the best memories of my wedding day. Every young woman who dreams of being a bride should have the same gift of doing it her way. Credit for that goes to my mother, who allowed me to be in charge of realizing my vision but helped with every part of the preparations. I promised myself that if I ever had daughters, I would do exactly the same for them.

The only note of sadness was that my father wasn't there to give me away. But it was nonetheless memorable and meaningful when Bernard Joseph Davisson II—my brother B.J., aged thirteen—walked me down the aisle and gave me away.

I have heard many brides admit that they weren't able to enjoy or remember much of the details of their weddings, for all kinds of reasons. Fortunately, that wasn't a problem for me. I soaked up every moment, cherishing the love and celebration that everyone seemed to heap on us. Maybe I'd already learned how important it was to make sure I'd taken care of everything in advance so I was then able to relax. And if anything wasn't just right, I wasn't paying attention and I wasn't looking back. My focus was only on the future and on making decisions about twists and turns in the road that were coming up for Fred and me—questions and considerations we hadn't necessarily anticipated as newlyweds.

The first order of business for each of us was to find jobs. After that we could figure out where we would live. In the meantime, we moved back into the house where I'd grown up. That was interesting, to say the least. Mom wanted to help and thought it was a fine idea. When I argued that we would be an added burden, she insisted that we would be a help to her in keeping up with Amy and B.J.

My first job out of college was teaching evening sewing classes at Sears, Roebuck in Cumberland. Fred and I were substitute teachers at Bruce High School, but those calls were intermittent. My preference would have been teaching school full-time but there were no job openings in either home economics or science. So I kept putting out feelers and considering any possibilities that were viable. Donna, who at that time met and soon married her husband, David Rea, a Baptist minister, was working in Harford County north of Baltimore and thriving. At the time the big city seemed like another world to me, but when Fred and I realized how stifling it was to keep living at my mother's home (or spending time at his mother's house), the idea of moving away was no longer so overwhelming.

When the opportunity arose for Fred to follow his dream to try out for the World Football League in Canada, I sent him off with my best hopes, thinking that up north would be an exciting change of pace. That position didn't pan out, but his next shot was a tryout with the Washington Redskins. Fred came close, making it past all the cuts and down to the last several players. But when the Redskins narrowed their choices to who would make the team, he wasn't among them. These disappointments certainly weighed heavily on him when he returned to Westernport to come up with plan B. This was a blow, and I understood that.

Coming from a positive place, I pointed out to him that it was better to have tried and not made it than to have never tried at all. I don't know if he agreed deep down or not. What I can say is that he didn't dwell on the disappointment for long and instead embraced his other interest—law enforcement—with a goal of eventually becoming an FBI agent.

After a year of living back at home, I was eager for the two of us to get out on our own. The time at home had given me more security, and it had been great to watch my mother balance her role as head of a household responsible for two teenagers with being a full-time teaching assistant. She also loved being in love and needed a man in her life. Not only that, but she had a definite preference for good-looking, athletic men. In fact, one of my most vivid memories of the time we lived in her house is that Mom put up a life-size poster of none other than Mark Spitz! After he won seven gold medals in swimming events at the 1972 Olympic Games in Munich, Leoma Davisson became an ardent fan. Little did we know he would play a peripheral role in our lives in the years to come.

During this era, Mom began a lovely relationship with a gentle-man whose attentions gave her a second youth that was a joy to see. It also put my mind at rest about deciding that Fred and I needed to move away. At twenty-three years old, I finally felt I had outgrown the Tri-Towns.

With no certain plan in mind, Fred and I agreed that who-ever received the first job offer—after months of sending out applications—would determine where we were heading. Lo and behold, an opening came up for a middle school home economics teacher in Havre de Grace in Harford County. Totally by coinci-dence, I would be starting my teaching career employed by the same county where Donna was working. Not long after I learned that I'd been hired for the position, Fred was accepted at the police academy not too far away in Pikesville. We were off and running.

I felt alive and excited that we were beginning married life under our own roof and that I'd be working in the classroom at last. The community of Havre de Grace, situated close to the water about forty-five minutes from Baltimore, had been going through a tran-sition in demographics. For many years, the school had been serv-ing mostly children from military families but recently there had been an increase in African American and Hispanic students whose families were moving out from the city to less populated suburbs.

When I arrived, the home economics department wasn't func-tioning sufficiently. There were two teachers—one who was African American and a mature, experienced teacher, while the other was white, with less experience and free-spirited. The expectation was that I would somehow mediate between these two. It was a tall or-der but I made it work just by throwing myself into the projects and engaging the students in them too. I was grateful for the demands on my time, particularly at first when Fred was required to stay overnight at the police academy in Pikesville during the week and could come home only on weekends. This meant that I found myself as a newlywed on my own much of the time. Initially it was touch-and-go, as I tried to build up a sense of security at being in a new city in a new job, not to mention that I was in a new apartment on the ground level with a husband away at the police academy. A lot of the challenge was psychological—just getting past my fear. In time, it was empowering to arrive at a place where I toughened up and realized I could fend for myself, while still looking forward to the weekend.

The students at this school had many needs. Some lacked the basic stability and security important for learning. Many were coping with stresses that were beyond the scope of my experience at that time. Many also came from cultural backgrounds different from my own. This was when it first occurred to me that in all my years growing up in Westernport, there had been only one black family in town, and their son Arnie had been the only minority student in my class. Arnie later became a prominent doctor and author—a hometown friend who had done well. That was the extent of my exposure to diversity growing up.

During my early months on the new job, I was shocked when a fourteen-year-old middle schooler stood next to me and said quite quietly and clearly, "I'd like to get you in bed." By reflex, I elbowed him in the ribs. Later I'd learn that that wasn't the way to handle such comments. And I'd also learn that from a cultural standpoint, he was just repeating what he'd heard other men in his neighborhood bragging about or saying about their conquests. I wasn't quite old enough to be his mother but it was no less shocking. After that, I made sure I had a fast comeback to inappropriate comments that were directed not just toward me but to other students and teachers.

As always, it was my belief that a child is a child and that understanding who he is has nothing to do with the color of his skin. At the same time, I wanted to know what motivated my students or limited them. If that meant I needed to become more culturally aware, I was happy to do so. I remember that this was a time when dashikis were all the rage for my African American students, so I decided we'd make them in my class as a sewing project. Dashikis are traditional African garments worn by men, like a tunic, made of beautiful, bright, colorful fabric with V-shaped necklines and could be made to fit tightly or more loosely. One of the eighth graders who wasn't enrolled in home economics kept begging to come to my class so he could get in on the action. As an incentive to do well in his English class, the deal was that he would be allowed to make a dashiki if he fulfilled his reading requirements.

The plan worked. He was enormously proud of the dashiki he designed and made. He and I also had a very positive connection in the process, and I had high hopes he had learned something of value.

After he went off to high school, from time to time I'd hear reports about how he was doing and was alarmed when the news came back that he was convicted of a violent offense and sent to prison. It didn't make sense. Why? He was basically a good young man, with a wonderful personality and a great smile. These questions didn't upset me as much as they challenged me to look for solutions.

Fred often told me I was far too idealistic, too eager to make a difference and save all the children and fix all the problems.

"You don't know how the real world works" was one of his popular refrains. "Debbie," he'd tell me whenever I sounded too naïve, "you're living in a bubble."

In his training and early work as a policeman, he would come home to tell me some of the horrors he was facing in law enforcement. "You don't know what's going on out there," Fred would say, not so much to chastise my lack of knowledge as to vent.

I knew people were being stabbed; I knew people were being shot. But I didn't have to play into that or glorify his hardships. That was his culture, the path he chose. Meanwhile, I was in a culture, a profession that was about the enhancement and enrichment of children—helping them grow into productive citizens. I was sympathetic to his reality, at least to the extent that I didn't want to be a policeman and go through their ordeals, to live in their world.

As time went on, I would have much more to say about the toll police work takes on the family—at least in our experience. But I was happy Fred had passion for his job. He was on the SWAT team in those years, the first man through the door, putting himself in the line of fire. When he segued to his path with the Maryland state police, I certainly saw him going far. He had the talent and drive, no question. But Fred bridled at working his way up the chain of command by the book. By his own admission, he didn't like to "kiss ass." His idea was to buck the system, or do it his own way. Compared to other cadets out of the police academy who had no college credits but were willing to work their way up, he had many advantages coming in with four plus years of college—not to mention charisma and communication skills.

My attitude for myself was that working your way up, putting in your time, had its rewards because you were always learning, always pushing yourself. But then again, for a state trooper who would rise to the level of corporal and even sergeant, maybe that wasn't how the real world worked.

Nineteen seventy-seven was a banner year for many reasons. It was a time of growth for Fred and me as husband and wife. We were both engaged in our careers and starting to see new horizons that we'd never imagined before. He had graduated from the state police academy and we had bought our first home, a modest but secure little place that I decorated on a budget, of course, and that we made into a charming abode. I really loved life!

The same pride that I'd once felt in coming from the Tri-Towns was now deepening into a love for the history and heritage of our home state; I became familiar with the diverse, distinctive traits that make Maryland, small as she is, what I consider to be America in the miniature. Down toward the bottom of the fifty states in terms of size (forty-second), Maryland nonetheless encompasses a broad range of geographical terrain, from the mountains in the western part of the state to the beaches at the eastern shore, from the small mining and farm communities to the urban centers like Baltimore and the suburbs surrounding Washington, D.C.

Here too, as when I was younger, I appreciated the differences in the seasons that could be experienced across the state. I definitely came to agree with whoever coined the slogan "Maryland is made for memories." As a teacher of home economics, I felt it was important to expand the concept of home not only to include household but also to encompass wherever we study, work, and live. The more I learned and felt passionate about our home state, the more I could share those discoveries with my students.

True, it might not have mattered to them at the time to be told that "The Star Spangled Banner" had been written by Francis Scott Key in Maryland during the War of 1812 as he witnessed the battle at Fort McHenry when the British failed to capture the port of Baltimore. But years later, whenever the national anthem was sung at meaningful events in their lives, I was sure they would feel added pride in knowing that the "dawn's early light" and the "rocket's red glare" had occurred on our soil.

In many ways, our state can claim status as the ultimate melting pot—and not just for cooking up our world-famous Maryland blue crabs from the Chesapeake Bay, where Baltimore and Annapolis sit. It's about the mix in our backgrounds, our seasonings. Maybe that's why Fred used to say, when asked about his heritage, that he was Heinz 57, comparing himself to the fifty-seven different seasonings in that famous sauce.

As it so happens, Maryland was the second most heavily trafficked point of entry for immigrants, who created diverse neighborhoods throughout the state in years to come. From my perspective, I was seeing firsthand that Marylanders could be both traditional and forward-thinkers, concerned about the betterment of themselves while also caring about the greater good. The Baltimore accent can be heard as a potpourri of influences—those from the South, because of Maryland's shared borders with the states of Virginia and West Virginia, plus those from the neighboring northeastern states of Delaware and Pennsylvania, as well as D.C. And since we had long been a gateway for pioneers moving to the Midwest and West, in my opinion we also represented the launching pad toward new frontiers.

Growing up, I had always loved the beauty of our state symbols that I saw in our midst—our state flower, the black-eyed susan (which some call the "girl next door" of flowers), and our state tree, the proud and determined white oak. As a young adult making headway in my teaching career, I had greater appreciation for the rich history of such other symbols as our state flag, with its four-checkered square of red, white, gold, and black, a pattern based on the coat of arms belonging to both the paternal and maternal family lines of George Calvert, the first Lord Baltimore, who founded what became the colony of Maryland in the early 1600s. I loved the fact that it was the only state flag in the nation to draw from the part of our history that dated back to families of nobility and their coats of arms established in British heraldry. It seemed all the more fitting that nature had endowed our state bird, the Baltimore oriole, with mainly black and gold feathers. Amazing!

The only state symbol that I wasn't sure about for some time was our motto, which came from our state seal. According to early translations it means "Manly Deeds, Womanly Words," which would later be revised to "Strong Deeds, Gentle Words." In any case, it suggested the balancing act required of all those who strive for greatness.

When the 1977 school year came to an end, Fred insisted that we get away on a vacation to Disney World. After we drove down to Florida and made it into the amusement park, standing in the hot summer sun, dripping from the humidity, I realized that I didn't feel very well and couldn't enjoy myself on the rides; they nauseated me.

That part wasn't fun, but it provided us with the very clue we needed to figure out that I was pregnant! I was in heaven, even with the initial queasiness, which soon went away. Everything about impending motherhood was joyous. I loved shopping for all the adorable baby items and, of course, putting together cute maternity outfits that I made or was able to buy economically. Fortunately, I was able to take excellent care of myself and had an easy, enjoyable pregnancy. And indeed in the months leading up to my due date of March 28, 1978, I read everything in print that was available at the time.

I had practically memorized Dr. Spock and had perused several baby name books before we were able to narrow down our options. Naturally, if we had a boy he was going to be named Michael Fred Phelps II. It was mentioned to me at some point that this was not precise etiquette unless there was a long lineage; actually, the naming would make my husband a Senior and my son the Junior. I could just imagine the teasing suffered by any child growing up with a Junior stuck on his name—along the lines of "Pee-Wee" or snide references to "little Junior," so it was a given that if we had a son, he would be called Michael to give him his own identity.

Fred agreed, as he usually did when I felt strongly about something, "Yes, Debbie, you're right. Whatever you say." Now, that was easy!

Coming up with a name for a girl was altogether different. Fred—who was undoubtedly expecting a boy—leaned toward some of the more masculine names that could go for girls. Many of them had heroic rings to them, like the name Hillary, which was inspired by Sir Edmund Hillary, the mountaineer who became the first climber to reach the summit of Mount Everest. We loved that, but I suggested we drop one of the *l*s because I didn't want the nickname Hill, as in a rolling mountain. But then again, I loved the name Megan, sweet-sounding but not too girlie, with roots in the Irish and Scottish heritage of our family. Then I went back and forth over middle names and resulting initials. For Hilary, we settled on the middle name Kristin, as it would give a strong monogram of HKP, and for Megan the middle name that jumped out at us was Jill, making the initials MJP.

The more I thought about it, the more Megan Jill grew on me. Fred was pleased either way, saying, "Whatever you choose, Debbie." After all, the girl name was more or less a backup, since everyone else's gut instincts told them we were having a boy. I was the only one who didn't have any clue—and knew that I was going to be thrilled no matter what.

By late morning on March 16, twelve days before my due date, a heavy snow began to fall and school closed early. Never one to sit still with free time on my hands, I decided—not surprisingly—to do some sewing and make, of all things, linen napkins.

So there I am making an elegant linen napkin when I have a contraction or at least believe that I do. How exciting, I think; the baby is going to come! Not wasting a second, I called Fred to come home from work and take me to the hospital.

Just as excited, he promised to hurry and showed up in record time with the police car, my official chariot. He dashed in the door, picked up my packed suitcase, and escorted me out through the falling snow in the gathering darkness. Opening the door for me on the front passenger side, he gently helped me into the car, and then, unable to resist the drama, pulled open the door to the backseat and threw my suitcase in with such force that it landed on top of his Stetson—and promptly squashed it. This was about to become a Phelps tradition, unintentionally, for all three children.

Fred was in his element, speeding onto the freeway to the hospital, wanting to set the lights flashing and with the siren ready to blare.

"Oh, my goodness, Fred!" I laughed. I had to convince him that the contractions weren't coming close enough together to warrant the lights and the siren. He was terribly disappointed, not to mention that he was planning on riding down the shoulder if need be. Nonetheless, when we arrived at the hospital, he gallantly made sure that I was seen without delay. He believed that a policeman's wife and family should benefit from the services provided to other citizens by law enforcement every day of the week.

Even though the doctors determined that I was nowhere near ready to deliver, they decided to keep me there—perhaps on account of the snow—and I proceeded to be in labor for the whole night. Exhausted, I was finally able to go to sleep for a few hours and woke up on the morning of March 17, Saint Patrick's Day. In this Catholic hospital, the first thing I heard echoing down the hallways was the sound of "When Irish Eyes Are Smiling," playing festively on the sound system.

At the same time, the doctors thought my labor was so long because the baby was too big for my size; they needed to see an X-ray. They had to take me down to the X-ray room, since the equipment in 1978 was too cumbersome to bring to me. In the elevator, a woman who worked in the hospital asked, "So, what names do you have picked out for your baby?"

I gave her the same response I'd been giving everyone, that if it was a boy, he would be Michael Fred. "If it's a girl, the names are Megan and Hilary."

"Oh, yes," she said, "you know we've been having Megans left and right in the nursery."

Well, that settled it. My first thought was, *If it's a girl, she's definitely not going to be a Megan.*

And sure enough, several hours later, still on Saint Patrick's Day, at 10:28 p.m., I gave birth to Hilary Kristin Phelps, weighing in at a very healthy nine pounds. The doctors finally decided to use forceps to pull her out, figuring that she was just so content inside, she wanted to stay there.

Fred now had his very own Daddy's little girl, and he was as thrilled as I was. Although in my delirious state, I did say to him, "I'm so sorry we didn't have a boy so you could take him fishing."

We both agreed that it was just one more reason to continue to grow as a family and have another baby—a brother for Hilary.

My mother was overjoyed to welcome her first grandchild into the world. She couldn't wait to start teaching Hilary to play the piano, convinced the child was musically inclined even as an infant.

Like her namesake, the explorer who first reached the summit of Mount Everest, Hilary Kristin Phelps was destined to be the family trailblazer—a seeker of knowledge, a risk taker, loving, resilient, always looking out for others, determined to save the world, a beauty, popular and high-spirited, and a diplomat. Yes, in the tradition of setting high standards and expectations that she was carrying on, she proved even as a baby to be ready for the challenge. And on her own terms, as a child born on Saint Patrick's Day—which she would celebrate in her first year of college, much to my initial chagrin, by getting on a whim a small, tasteful tattoo of a shamrock—she definitely had the luck of the Irish on her side and on the side of those she most cared about.

FOUR

~~~~

Growing Pains

Not too long after Hilary was born, I was offered a timely opportunity to teach at North Harford Middle School, which was being opened by Harry Hinman, my former assistant principal from Havre de Grace. When he was promoted to principal and given this school in northern Harford County, I was eager to follow him both for the advancement and for the challenge. North Harford was in a more rural area, and most of the students were the children of parents who worked in agriculture, many who were nicknamed "duck farmers." That was definitely a change of pace, with new students from different backgrounds to get to know. Changes bring challenges, which I knew would allow me to grow, as would the freedom that Mr. Hinman gave me to design and run my classroom and the entire home economics department in a way that honored the subject matter and the students. I wanted to have the food preparation and projects going on in one area, with sewing projects in a second area, and this worked beautifully. The energy and excitement in the classroom allowed me to feel I was accomplishing my goal not just of being a good teacher but also of reaching for greatness. It was around this time that I stopped using the word "good" for goals and instead replaced it with "great."

And on that note, going into the fall of 1979, there was more great news: we were expecting our second child. Once again, I savored the experience of looking forward to whoever the next marvelous human being would be. As with my first, this pregnancy was smooth sailing, and I was able to work full-time in the classroom, confident that Hilary was in excellent hands at a day care center close to where we lived.

And the whole naming process required less research this time around. For a boy we had Michael Fred ready to go, no debate. For a girl, our challenge was to top or rival a name that was associated with Mount Everest. The obvious choice was Mount Whitney, the highest peak in the United States. The name Whitney had a wonderful ring to it, and I loved it right away. The only challenge was finding a middle name that rolled off the tongue with the right music. I'm not sure how Nikol with that spelling arose, but that was the pick—Whitney Nikol.

A day before my due date, on the evening of April 14, 1980, we were invited to a party at the home of Hilary's nursery school teacher. It was a warm gathering, and I was happy that Fred and I could attend together, since his schedule at work was sometimes prohibitive when it came to social events. Even though I hadn't felt many signs that the baby was soon to arrive, I suddenly felt huge. In fact, I turned to Fred at a certain point and said, "You know, I feel like my insides are about to fall out."

Before either of us could hem and haw too much, we called my ob-gyn, who told us to hurry to the hospital. One of my closest friends, who was at the party, immediately volunteered to watch Hilary for as long as we needed.

Fred was back in his element, taking charge, somehow managing yet again to open the car's back door dramatically and throw in a bag that smashed his Stetson a second time. No lights or siren were needed at this time of night, but I was relieved that Fred was able to get us there as fast as he did, because when we pulled up to the emergency entrance and they put me in the wheelchair, the contractions were coming quickly, one after the other. When the people at the desk insisted that I fill out my paperwork, I had to tell them that if they didn't wheel me in, the baby was going to be born in the waiting room.

It was almost that fast too. Compared to my first, epic labor, this was zip, zip, zap, and Whitney Nikol Phelps—weighing in at 9 lbs., 4 oz.—made her grand entrance into the world. The time was 4:48 a.m. on April 15, tax day, her actual due date.

As for the boy we were still hoping to have, Fred and I agreed that number three would be the charm. Meanwhile our new charmer Whitney captivated our attention. A joy and a live wire, from the moment of her arrival Whitney was her own person, with limitless energy, boundless curiosity, and a desire to do everything her sister was already doing.

As I remember my early days of motherhood, I can see that with each baby, I loved the next baby that much more—knowing how quickly each stage would come and go. It seems strange to see it that way, but I can recall that as much as I held each one, I held the next one that much more. I loved Hilary and cuddled her with all my heart, concerned, however, about whether I was doing everything right—by the book. There were checkpoints that I was looking for, as if to say, "Okay, this is when you should be rolling over," and then, "You should be crawling now; why aren't you crawling?" or "Okay, time to walk now."

With Whitney, I was able to enjoy those stages with more ease, not worrying so much about the precise timeline. Not only was I more confident, but Whitney was following Hilary, accelerating her learning curve by having a big sister whose lead she could follow. It went that way for a while. I have memories of the three of us going to the grocery store and each of us pushing a separate cart. First I would have the Mom grocery cart, then Hilary came behind me with the little cart, and next there was Whitney with her cart toddling along behind Hilary. A trip to the grocery store was often a whole production.

As if there wasn't enough action already, we had another member of the household who wanted in on everything Hilary and Whitney were doing. That was our huge Saint Bernard named Hans Nanitchka—affectionately known as Nitchi—who of course had to have a distinguished name that paid homage to his breed's history of rescuing Alpine hikers and skiers. Nitchi even had a barrel that we put under his chin.

When Whitney was born, Hans Nanitchka would put his large fluffy head at the side of the bed and Hilary would climb on top of him and get him to lie down. The antics among the three of them kept us in stitches constantly.

It didn't take long for us to decide that we needed a bigger house. After we purchased five acres of wooded property, there wasn't enough money from our joint savings to build right away, and I hadn't gone back to work yet. Our plan was to build our expansive, gorgeous dream home there eventually. We opted to set up a decent-sized trailer that would be our living accommodations while construction was taking place. The reality I faced within a few years was that the job of overseeing the construction of a home and raising two little girls, now aged five and three, with a husband working varied shifts as a policeman, would be a full-time undertaking. After much deliberation, I decided not to go back to teaching while we were building the house, but once it was built, I'd open up my own day care.

Everything seemed to be falling into place for us to forge ahead, all systems go. We had bought the trailer, moved into it on the five acres out in the middle of nowhere, and settled in. Not long after I had started to meet with the architect, Fred informed me that, after much thought, he felt he needed to have some more space, and he was moving out.

At first, and for a short period, I assumed that this was a midlife crisis, perhaps an early case of it, and that it was understandable because our growing household and responsibilities were putting pressure on him, on top of the stress of his job.

I thought of the demands on him from his night shifts and the constant rotation of hours that police work required, combined with how I'd gotten so busy—teaching Sunday school, being so involved with the girls, taking on added duties like being a Brownie leader, focusing on building the house, expanding our horizons—and yet I still couldn't figure out why on earth he could need more space. Was I being too demanding, too needy, too dependent? Well, no, I concluded, not at all.

Then I was told there was someone else in the picture.

Well, as upsetting as that was for me to hear, it helped me to see the reality of the situation. So, rather than tear myself up anymore, I decided to go and find out what was going on—to look Fred in the eyes and know in my heart whether this was temporary or if he was really ready to give up on what we were building together.

When I tracked him down, there were plenty of questions that I could have asked, but all I needed to do was to look at him. By the uncomfortable expression on his face, I had my answer. Not one word was spoken, but the silence told me that he wasn't planning on coming home anytime soon.

We could have sat down and had a long, anguished conversation, but that wasn't our style. Instead I turned right around and walked away quickly.

From where I am today, thanks to the passage of time, combined with twenty-twenty hindsight and the relationship lessons that others have generously shared with me over the years, I can honestly say I'm grateful for what I learned during that terribly trying time. For one thing, I learned that you never know how strong or determined you really are until you're put into a situation where you either sink or swim. Not a bad metaphor to take me into the next chapters of my life. For another thing, I had to learn that even when you are singing Helen Reddy's song "I Am Woman (Hear Me Roar)"—that is, no matter how strong, determined, and resilient you are—when someone you love does something that hurts you, well, plain and simple, it hurts.

Heading into the fall of '83 after we separated, I was still in a state of shock. It didn't make sense. For months, I racked my brain trying to replay conversations and events that might provide clues as to what had gone wrong. Or, as I tended to ask, what had I done wrong? Was I that naïve? After all, I'd always thought we were the perfect family. I had thought that everything was great. Our children, two beautiful girls, ages three and five, were the greatest, and our lives were filled with meaningful and fun experiences. Wasn't that everything a family was supposed to be?

I decided at some point that perhaps the problem was that we didn't have a boy yet. I knew Fred had been yearning for a son. Then again, I only had to look at the closeness between my father and me to see that, clearly, girls can be as close to their dads as boys.

I kept looking for how I had failed. Maybe I'd been misguided in my attempts to be the ideal wife and mother—trying to present myself in a way that was attractive and appropriate for a relatively young woman of thirty-two, being a loving presence in my daughters' lives, excelling in my work, teaching Sunday school, being a Brownie leader. I thought that was what all mothers did.

It was easier to think that somehow the fault was mine, because that meant if I used my problem-solving skills, I could figure out how to fix it. The truth that would take me many more years to understand was much more complicated. Later I would accept that Fred and I were both changing but in different ways. As a result we had new sets of issues we were not prepared to handle or address.

In the beginning, as I could well remember, Fred had been so accommodating, just agreeing and going along with the game plan that mostly I directed, with his "Yes, Debbie," and "whatever you want, Debbie." When that got old for him, as it probably did, he didn't know how to put the brakes on or how to disagree in a constructive way. Instead he said little, and resentment may have built up. And some men who are used to being the center of attention when it comes to the woman in their life have a hard time taking a backseat to their children.

That doesn't mean I would have changed anything about how I tried to find balance by throwing myself into every aspect of our lives. Yes, I wanted to do more, learn more, grow more, to push ourselves to the next place—and to be happy, happy doing it! Fred got to a point, I suspect, where he just wanted to *be*.

Once during Christmastime, as I was busy decorating the tree, wrapping presents, and stringing up lights, and he was sitting on the sofa watching TV, I remember him saying, "If you tie one more bow or hang one more wreath, I'm going to go crazy."

And then there was the time when the girls were asleep and we sat down to watch a movie on TV. We hadn't been watching long when I found myself getting up from time to time—tidying here and there, making sure items were ready for packing lunches for the morning, grabbing the laundry basket to fold clothes as we continued to watch.

Fred said, "Do you have to do that?"

I didn't see the big deal. Besides, I couldn't just sit and watch TV without doing something with my hands.

He should have known me well enough by then, but he had to ask, "Can't you just focus on me and the movie?"

I laughed because he hadn't meant it in any mean way. But my laughter masked the realization that he probably would have preferred that I not be so busy all the time. It was a signal that we were moving into uncharted waters as a couple when we discovered we had different priorities and lifestyle needs. Where he was content to be passive and stick with the status quo, I wanted us to set our sights much higher. Then it occurred to me that he was still struggling over the fact that his dreams of playing professional sports hadn't panned out.

Rather than being mad, I was embarrassed at being a failure. And I was supposed to be an expert in family! For that reason, I spoke to almost no one about what was going on. Of those who knew, everyone assured me that things would work out between Fred and me. This was only temporary, they said, and everyone agreed that all marriages hit rough patches. My mother and my sister Donna, always supportive, comforted me by saying that everything was going to be all right. Mom told me knowingly, "Don't worry, he'll come back." Whether or not I believed that, I reminded myself how she had risen to the challenge after Dad passed away, and that became the inspiration I needed to get out of my funk.

Since I had always been athletic, I started the process by working out at the gym, and I threw myself into aerobics with a passion, soon finding myself in the best shape of my life. When a position teaching aerobics became available, I thought that I'd be a shoo-in. After all, I was an experienced teacher and had a background as a cheerleader. What better skills for motivating others and cheering them on? To my dismay, I was not selected for the position. My aerobics instruction dreams were instantly dashed! But on a more hopeful note, when it became necessary that I return to work, I struck gold as soon as I reached out to colleagues in the school system, letting them know I was back in the job market.

Within no time, I was hired as a teacher at Southampton Middle School. It was in a somewhat more affluent community than where I'd worked previously, with what was considered a higher-achieving student body, not too far from where we were living. I felt great getting back to the classroom in a new setting with a new atmosphere.

No matter what demographic the children happened to come from, I learned from every setting where I taught. While the specific issues might be different, depending on family income, cultural background, and so on, what I learned from my students is that with structure, encouragement, attention, and care, children will thrive and push themselves. I was already seeing that lesson in action with Hilary as she started school and with Whitney, who was still in day care.

Slowly, step by step, the lemons-into-lemonade part of myself rose once again. I wasn't quite the old version of happy-happy all the time, especially when winter came and I had to deal with no water out on the five acres in the middle of nowhere, plus frozen pipes in the trailer. That was character-building, as they say!

Unlike my mom, who was buoyed so much by her social life when she was newly single, during this time I didn't feel the need to date or socialize more to raise my spirits. To the contrary, I bene-fited from time spent alone—getting to know myself in ways I never had before. I've heard similar stories from others, both women and men, who have experienced such growing pains after suddenly finding themselves alone.

As unpleasant as these passages can be, I can vouch for the fact that they are necessary, as Dr. Seuss describes in *Oh, the Places You'll Go!*, one of my all-time favorite books. Dr. Seuss tells us that "You'll play lonely games," but that's part of life and learning, and that "on you will go." And he promises we will succeed—"You will indeed!"

Alone was something I accepted as a part of life, something I experienced in a profound way for the first time in my life. After almost a year without Fred, what seemed like an eternity, I took my wedding band off and tucked it away in a ring box in my dresser. I had no sooner done that, and even begun to prepare myself for the next steps, when what do you know? Fred showed up unannounced, acknowledged he had made a mistake, and asked me to take him back. And I did.

FIVE

For Better and for Worse

No matter how many times I'm asked if there was anything early on about Michael that indicated he was born to swim—with the perfect physiology for the sport that he is said to have—my answer is an honest no. I have also said that with his natural athleticism, competitive drive, and tenacious work ethic, he would have excelled at whatever sport he'd chosen to compete in.

All of that said, I remember that in the last month of my pregnancy, Michael's feet kept pushing against my side—something I hadn't experienced with either Hilary or Whitney. I think he needed more room to stretch out to his full length. Even before he made his entry into the world, he was a very active baby with those feet of his, flutter kicking away inside me. Maybe that was a clue after all.

By spring 1985, with our third child due in July, life had returned to the normal nonstop action for our family. The first thing Fred and I had decided to do upon his return was to go forward with building our dream house, as we'd originally planned. I'm not sure he was as passionate about it as I was, but it allowed the two of us to focus on all kinds of practical questions, as opposed to spending too much time dwelling on our time apart.

All in all, it was a hopeful season for new beginnings that looked promising. It wasn't in my nature to expect things not to work out. True, I wasn't wearing the same rose-colored glasses I had worn in the past, but just as with my two girls, I was in happy-happy expectant mother mode, participating in the greatest creative act in life.

Not that we had any concrete reasons for being sure that the baby on the way was definitely going to be a boy, but we had a strong feeling. I say this because even as we got closer to July, the only name we had picked out was Michael Fred Phelps. Michelle was the only backup name that I had seriously considered in the event we ended up having a girl.

The one thing that was close to certain was that our third child was destined to be born on July 4, his due date. Since that was the family tradition, with Hilary born on Saint Patrick's Day and Whitney on April 15, tax day, it was practically a given that our third would top those entrances and arrive with a splash on Independence Day 1985.

But getting into the last days of June, I started to think that maybe we weren't going to make it that far. Summer had arrived with rising heat and off-the-chart humidity, not to mention that I'd grown out of my maternity tops and shorts for hot weather. So on Friday, June 30, I went to see my wonderful ob-gyn for a checkup. She was one of my few confidantes in those days, and as it happened, we shared a number of things because we were both career women and were both married to policemen.

My friend and physician said, "Debbie, the baby is coming this weekend."

"Okay," I said, thinking maybe I could just hold out until the fourth. I silently admitted to being disappointed that we wouldn't be able to do stars and stripes on birthday cakes and such. (Little did I know.)

"The only thing is," she added, "I'm going sailing this weekend. I won't be here for the delivery. The on-call doctor will deliver, unless you want to do it now."

"Let's go," I said, and decided to go straight from her office to the hospital to induce labor.

Somehow, once again, Fred followed tradition with his flair for drama by hurrying me into the car, throwing open the backseat, tossing my things in, and squashing his Stetson. And once again, he didn't get to put on his siren, flash his lights, or drive down the shoulder of the freeway. What did happen this time, as you probably already know, was that the name Michael Fred Phelps finally greeted the bouncing baby boy we had been saving it for. Born that same Friday, June 30, 1985, Michael came in at a whopping 9 lbs., 6 oz., ready to hold his own and follow in the footsteps of his active, energetic older sisters, Hilary, age seven, and Whitney, age five.

As babies, each of my three had their own personalities, without a doubt, but Michael was almost like having a first child all over again because he was a male. He was a bundle of energy from the moment I first held him in my arms. Besides being so loving, sweet, funny, and happy, he also had a natural ability to put himself in the middle of the action, no matter what it was—a trait that I suppose hasn't changed much since then!

The arrival of Michael—as the boy Fred could soon take fishing and with whom he would share his passion for sports and all those other traditional father-son activities—seemed to usher in a memorably happy time for the whole family. Admittedly, before he was born, there were still undercurrents of tension between Fred and me, mostly because I couldn't really trust him and because I was constantly worried that I wasn't doing everything to make sure that what had gone wrong before wouldn't happen again.

I now realize that I wasn't being fair to myself. This is the point I often make to women who share my habit of assuming that we're responsible as wives, women, and moms for making sure everything is perfect:

> Believe it or not, at the Olympics they don't give gold medals for Superwoman! And P.S., it's okay to be slightly less than perfect.

I hadn't exactly learned that lesson yet (I'm still working on it). In the meantime, having Michael in our lives gave me a wave of relief and relaxation that put my fears to rest. Naturally, I loved seeing Fred's delight, the glisten in those blue eyes of his that got me every time, his slow-spreading smile, and that genuine expression of joy that had been part of what had first drawn me to him in our teens. This relaxed atmosphere certainly helped keep the romance percolating between us even when we didn't see eye to eye about everything. Of course, I also loved watching Hilary and Whitney dote on their kid brother.

And so, the family—as busy as ever with the big house nearing completion and the onset of swimming lessons, dance, music, Brownies, and gymnastics—settled into a rhythm of normalcy, a kind of controlled, creative chaos. I found calm in the middle of it all, oddly enough, partly thanks to the calming effect that Michael had on me, even though he was a speedy, active boy baby, always on the go, constantly curious and unable to be still for long.

Wait. Did I just put the words "calming" and "Michael" in the same sentence? I'm not sure what it was, especially when he spent most of his toddlerhood in training for being underfoot as much as possible. But even early on, I could see there was a place of depth within him—an inner stillness that was destined to come to the surface at unpredictable moments. As Whitney later described it when he grew older, Michael has an uncanny ability to perform at the highest level of physical output and then to shift into his lowest gear, where, in her words, he could "just chill."

Then again, there was nothing calming about some memorably close calls we had when Michael was young.

Back when he was around two years old, our menagerie had grown to include the various animals Hilary had invited to join the family. A budding veterinarian in those days—with all sorts of science and chemistry studies that fascinated her too—she had started a collection of gerbils and other adopted pets that she could heal and care for. After our Saint Bernard Hans Nanitchka had gone missing (we suspected he was stolen), Fred brought home a German shepherd he had rescued from a farm while out on patrol.

The dog hadn't gotten along with the children at the farm, apparently. We assumed that that was because they had mistreated him. Fred said the dog had had a rag doll he had destroyed and torn up at his old home. To be safe, we kept him outside in a kennel, and he seemed to be adjusting to a loving environment. One day when Fred was sleeping inside and I was doing several things at once, Hilary went to feed the dog on her own. As usual, Michael went trailing after her. The moment she opened the kennel, the dog spotted this skinny little guy and mistook him for a rag doll.

The next thing we knew, the German shepherd had Michael by the collar of his jacket and was dragging him around the kennel, tossing him this way and that, rubbing his face in the dirt. Hilary screamed at the top of her lungs, and I rushed outside to see Michael on the ground. I scooped him up in my arms and ran into the house, carrying a panic-stricken little boy with pebbles pushed into his face and blood on him, yelling so loud about the deranged dog that I woke Fred. After filling up the bathtub with warm water and washing Michael clean, I was relieved that none of the bites were too deep. Needless to say, he survived. Still, Fred made it clear to the children that we had to get rid of the dog—something they didn't understand any more than why he would attack Michael in the first place. Michael had a series of rabies shots until clearance was given from the doctors that he was going to be all right.

Another six months passed before we had a scare that came close to that one. It happened during Christmas vacation, when

Mom had come up to spend the holidays with us. From the beginning, Gran and Michael were thick as thieves. A couple of years
later, she famously taught him to play cards, and he became so good
at games like 500 rummy and kings in the corner that in his teens,
whenever they played, she accused him of cheating.

Michael always hated to lose. Most children and adults, for that
matter, don't like to lose, but as his sisters and grandmother can attest, he turned hating to lose into an art form, starting in preschool.
Being the lady that my mother was, she never resorted to histrion-
ics. But she didn't like to lose either, so she and her grandson were
soul mates from the start.

One day during Gran's stay that Christmas, I noticed that Michael wasn't cuddling up with his grandmother or making an at-
tempt to hijack Whitney's presents as he normally would. When I
felt his forehead, he seemed a little warm, but I wasn't too concerned
at first. I decided to just keep an eye on him in case there was any
change.

We were waiting for Fred to return from his trip to Delaware,
where he had taken Hilary for a swim meet—an event that was
becoming more and more frequent. This was when I was having my
first inklings that we might need to move to Baltimore County, as
the kids were getting more involved in swimming. I really hadn't
expected it to become the focus of our lives. Besides being another
area of interest to add to the dance and music lessons, as a form of
enrichment, swimming had actually started as a suggestion from
our pediatrician, who believed in having children learn water safety
at a young age. It had been many months since Hilary convinced us
to move her to the training facilities for North Baltimore Aquatic

Club, where Whitney was also swimming now. When the idea that we might want to move closer to where they were training first hit me, I didn't jump right away. But the more I thought about it, the more it made sense.

Living out in the sticks at the northern edge of Harford County near the Pennsylvania state line, though not too far from the girls' school, Michael's day care, and the middle school where I taught, was an hour commute each way to the pools where NBAC training took place. This meant that many nights the girls were eating dinner in the minivan, sometimes even doing homework on the way there and back. Occasionally they had to be at two different locations at the same time for lessons and for meets.

These particulars were in my mind as I waited for Fred and Hilary to return from her meet. My idea was that if we sold our house and bought one in the vicinity of Towson, where the schools were great and the pools were nearby, the only commute would be my driving to my job and back. True, after we'd finally moved into the dream house we'd built, the decision to sell would be a tough call. But with all the commuting, we were hardly ever in this house.

I knew Fred wouldn't want to move. Being in Baltimore County would be city living, and he was much happier out in the country with our five acres of space and quiet. I was torn. On the one hand, as a wife, I wanted Fred to be happy. On the other, as a mother, I wanted the children to have our unconditional support that would allow them to throw themselves fully into whatever they loved. Sure, they could lose interest in swimming, and then we might regret the move. But my gut told me that wasn't going to happen.

The other concern was that these hours spent in various commutes were already starting to create distance between Fred and me. We were on the run so much that we were throwing kisses to each other in passing, racing out the door to work, getting the children to where they needed to go, sometimes waving at each other from our cars. We talked more on the telephone to coordinate drop-offs and pickups than we did in person. Not that our marriage was in trouble, or at least I didn't think it was. After all, I really did believe that regardless of past problems, we had committed for better and for worse. So I resolved to keep the faith and wait for a while before pushing for a move.

Faith was always important, whether in times of hope or uncertainty—like that day when I realized Michael's forehead was no longer just warm but was very hot with a fever that was spiking. By the time Fred and Hilary returned from the meet, I had already talked to our pediatrician, who was concerned enough to urge me to get Michael to the hospital right away.

That was one of the few times I was grateful that Fred could legally speed us to the hospital in his highway patrol car, using the lights and the siren. I knew he was also a great driver at that high speed, so I kept my composure as I held Michael in my arms in the front seat, telling myself the whole way that there was no cause for alarm.

The explanation for the sudden spike in fever that wasn't accompanied by other symptoms had to do with an imbalance in his white and red blood cells. We weren't sure what had happened to bring it on or why it was happening, but he was going to need to be admitted immediately.

It was not easy watching my little two-and-half-year-old with his long skinny limbs, dressed in his woolly blanket sleeper, curled up in a chair with IVs stuck into him and tubes connecting him to machines.

My worries were like those of all parents when their beloved child is hurting or sick. The other cause for worry had to do with my history. Except to give birth to my three children, I hadn't been in a hospital to visit a loved one since the night I said good-bye to my father. I had been devastated when I realized the doctors couldn't pull off a miracle for Dad. The more that stayed in my memory, the more fearful I became—knowing that Michael was burning up with fever, hearing his shallow breathing, seeing him struggle with the imbalance in his blood cells. I was grateful that Fred was there and we were going through this together. But I felt helpless.

My only resort was to pray silently, asking for the peace and strength that faith can bring. A quiet calm followed. I had a feeling that everything was going to be all right. The awareness came to me that there was a very strong spirit in that little boy lying there in the hospital, and he was going to get through this scare unscathed. And indeed, I was right.

As for my other fears about the security of my marriage and our family, I also had faith: whatever was going to be, for better and for worse, was going to be all right too.

~~~

SIX

It's in the Cards

In the years between 1987 and 1991, I was christened—so to speak—into a new kind of church that had no religious affiliation but indeed offered fellowship, inspiration, instruction, family and community connection, as well as responsibilities and obligations that included more hours wearing a chauffeur's hat than I could have predicted. Of course, I'm talking about the Phelps family's immersion into the world and culture of swimming, as practiced and mastered at the North Baltimore Aquatic Club.

Little did I know when we took Hilary and Whitney for their first visit to watch a major meet at Meadowbrook in the Mount Washington neighborhood of Baltimore County that swimming was about to become swimming the NBAC way. And the pool itself—wherever it was—was about to become home away from home and school away from school.

"I'm not swimming in that pool!" seven-year-old Whitney had exclaimed the moment she caught her first glimpse of the 50-meter long-course outdoor swimming pool at Meadowbrook, one of the two facilities where she and Hilary would practice most of the time.

Unlike the indoor 25-yard short-course pool at Loyola/Blakefield, NBAC's other main training facility in those days, Meadowbrook did not yet have an indoor swimming pool (as it does now). That wasn't Whitney's problem. Her issue was the length of the pool.

Nine-year-old Hilary wasn't concerned in the least. Since she had instigated the move to NBAC from where she had been swimming at RASAC (Renaissance All-Sports Athletic Club), her first glimpse of Meadowbrook was like seeing for herself the peaks of Mount Everest. Ready to set the world on fire, Hilary was just elated to be swimming on the same team with all the girls she'd been competing against.

Whitney didn't take any comfort from the awe-inspiring history of Meadowbrook's pool, which dated back to 1930. And at age seven, she wasn't especially wowed by the fact that swimmers from NBAC had qualified for the Olympics practically every four years since the club's founding in the late 1960s.

Whitney's little voice shook as she said, "I don't want to swim in that pool. It's too long!"

Not knowing what to say, I smiled and shrugged my shoulders with a glance at Murray Stephens, the head swim coach of Loyola Blakefield High School (as well as a prominent English professor at the private boys' prep school in Towson, some ten minutes north of downtown Baltimore). A cofounder of NBAC, he was its driving force—with both "driving" and "force" being operative. Before Murray could respond to Whitney, his wife, Patty, came over and waved away all worries, explaining, "Oh, we don't swim in that pool very often. Why don't you just come down and practice in the pool at Loyola. Don't worry about this pool."

With that, Whitney blinked away her tears, much relieved. Since our first several months with NBAC would be at Loyola in the 25-yard short-course pool during the fall, winter, and early spring, by summertime Whitney would have completely gotten past her fears of swimming the length of the 50-meter pool. Interestingly enough, it would turn out that she—like her sister and later her brother—could use the long course to her advantage.

The key difference happened to be with the turns. The short-course pools have more of them, of course, and as youngsters both Hilary and Whitney (and later Michael) weren't the most sensational with turns. Because 50-meter pools required fewer turns, the children could rely more on their strengths of endurance and stroke precision. They were also able to utilize the pool length to keep the rhythm going and thus increase their speed, whereas other swimmers needed the turns for added propulsion.

Let me quickly add that I'm speaking here as an observer and mother, not as an expert. Still, it would be fascinating to see how each of my children's learning curves were shaped by their older sibling—with Hilary, our navigator, leading the way, then Whitney, tenacious and determined, moving up the ranks even faster, and finally Michael, who would start out in a more leisurely fashion, mastering fundamentals, and then suddenly skyrocket to the loftiest heights. As he says, "No limits."

Certainly just as each child had his or her own personality and motivation, each had a distinct style as a swimmer that would become more marked over time. Early on there were similarities among all three—natural athleticism, above average amounts of competitive drive and focus, and a willingness to take the daily steps necessary for reaching their goals. The three Phelps swimmers even swam similar races in their younger years. For example, they were all 1500-meter freestylers, a cornerstone for endurance. Early on, all three were naturals in the butterfly—a rhythm, breathing, and power stroke. In my humble opinion, each of them was gifted in backstroke, although neither of the girls (nor Michael, for that matter, at least not yet) had enough opportunities to prove their talents in those particular events.

With all that noted, I still had to abide by one of the most important though sometimes unspoken "commandments" for all swim parents (or gung ho parents of children in any sport). As the mom on Team Phelps, I have come to pride myself on recognizing the clear delineation of roles for everyone involved, and often cite this rule for myself and when giving advice to others. There are exceptions, as we know, but for the most part if you're a parent with a child pursuing any form of athletics for fun, to improve skills, or to follow a dream, I do recommend keeping this one in your back pocket for easy access:

> Let coaches do the coaching.

Learning that simple lesson, even though I already agreed with it absolutely in theory, came to me in the form of baptism by fire. I remember having to bite my tongue when Hilary first tried on her NBAC swimsuit.

"What do you think, Mom?" she asked, modeling the blue, rounded-neck one-piece with goldenrod yellow piping.

Immediately I flashed on the first time I ever saw her compete, back in the bygone days of a summer league that had started her interest in swimming. Not only did I think she was the most competitive, but in that Hawaiian print, one-sided bathing suit, with the darling ruffle across the bodice, and no swim cap and no goggles, she was the most adorable child on the pool deck. Compared with the other swimmers at that meet, she looked tiny. But fearless and focused, Hilary wasn't intimidated whatsoever.

Now, standing in front of me in her NBAC official swimsuit, she had the same serious, fearless look of a competitor ready to prove herself. But boy, cute suits were now a thing of the past. Rather than give her my blunt opinion—that the uniforms weren't going to win "most attractive swim attire"—I gave her a hug, answering truthfully, "Oh, you're beautiful!"

The NBAC suits were clean, classic, and official-looking, and the colors matched the club's T-shirts, warm-up clothes, sweats, and bags. True, the other clubs in the late 1980s were wearing the newest, splashiest Speedos and various other designer brands with patterns and colors—much more eye-catching than the boring, not very flattering blue and gold uniforms that the powers that be had chosen. But as the elite top club, I figured NBAC was making a statement that it wasn't about the suits.

One of the only times I dared to approach a coach with a question was when we attended Hilary's first zone meet—in Hershey, Pennsylvania, home of the chocolate factory. This was a major rite of passage for age group swimmers, who usually had to qualify by swimming a time trial in order to go to meets called "zones" where they would be competing with their club and as part of a state delegation against qualifiers from the several states that were part of their zone. In Hilary's case, after as many as five attempts during a time trial opportunity to better her time in the 50-meter backstroke, she had made the cut to be eligible to go to the zone meet, where she would be competing with swimmers from states across the Eastern Zone—from Maine down to Virginia. This was the big time and we were all excited for her.

That is, until we arrived at the pool in Hershey and I could see, to my horror, that the pool was a mere four feet deep. All of a sudden I went from being the proud mother of a daughter who had qualified for her first zones in backstroke, to a very scared novice parent imagining her little girl diving into the water and bashing her head!

Unable to stop myself, I respectfully approached Tom Hines, NBAC's head age group coach, and said, "I don't mean to interfere and I know that I'm a new parent on the team and Hilary has not been training with you very long, but this pool is so shallow, I don't want her to dive too deep and crack her head open."

With kindness and patience, Tom immediately reassured me, "I understand and I'll take care of it. I'll make sure that Hilary is reminded. There's nothing you need to worry about."

Tom said all the right things, and I calmed down right away.

Even so, it wasn't until the race was over that I could completely relax.

Hilary didn't win her race or swim a memorable time—competing as she was with a more seasoned field—but it was at that zone meet that she ran out after her race to breathlessly inform me that she had seen something in the locker room that was very exciting.

"Mom," she whispered, coming up close to my ear to confide what it was, "some of the girls shave!"

In the locker room before the race, Hilary had witnessed one of the mothers shaving her daughter's back. At nine and ten years old, girls were usually just beginning to shave their legs, if that, but elite swimmers went further. Hilary thought that was just amazing and couldn't wait until she was at the level of serious competition at which every contender shaves every part of his or her body—backs, legs, arms, everywhere. We were definitely not in Kansas anymore.

Meanwhile, there was a learning curve for all of us as a swim family, starting with getting to know the seasonal structure of the swimming calendar. The big kickoff came every year with the Blue/Gold Meet—referring to NBAC's team colors—which signaled the end of summer and the launch of the fall season. Later updated and renamed Team Day, it included the Inner Squad Meet, with our swimmers competing against each other, and it was held in conjunction with a wonderful family picnic and an informative meeting to celebrate the beginning of a new season. You would meet the swimmers in the various levels, find out who your coach was going to be, and receive your bill for the season—an annual ritual.

In concert with the onset of fall and the new school year, practice sessions began in earnest at the Loyola pool. The 25-yard short-course pool that was part of the Loyola/Blakefield campus had its own prestigious and impressive history. Still, the first plunge in the pool for the season was a reminder of the hard work ahead. In those days, before a later remodeling was undertaken, there was nothing very glamorous about the facility. Aging and dingy, with paint peeling from the walls, not only did it smell of the chlorine that was in the water, but its locker rooms and hallways carried whiffs of chlorinated days of yore. That smell was destined to become familiar to every dedicated swimmer. Usually, the short-course competitive season—where meets were swum in yards, not meters—would correspond with the rest of the school year calendar.

In swimming terms, the month of May signified that it was soon time to move to Meadowbrook for practice and competition. Every year the swimmers and their families anticipated the first day at the outdoor long-course pool with excitement and trepidation. This event never ceased to be a big deal for everyone. Invariably, no matter how warm the weather had been in the weeks leading up to the first May date at Meadowbrook, the day always turned out to be misty and cold, and the first leap into the water was bone-chilling. The weather in Maryland is hard to predict, so even with a heated pool, this shock was just a given.

Many memories of this time of year take me back to driving over there at the crack of dawn to watch the swimmers gather for morning warm-ups in late spring and summer. Steam would be rising from the water. You could almost see the heat coming from the swimmers' bodies as they dove in without complaint, beginning their drills, focused and intent, everyone seemingly immune to the cold water or just feeling good to know they were in the happening place to be! Indeed, serious contenders came to train not only from the Baltimore area but from miles away—Delaware, New York, and beyond. NBAC was that prestigious.

There was a kind of unspoken indoctrination process for new swim parents that involved letting us know this was a no-nonsense training ground for excellence, coupled with very high expectations. It was clear, however, with the foundation that was to be gained at North Baltimore, that there were many roads to be followed. One avenue could be pursued mainly for recreation; yet another could lead toward collegiate swimming and competition; another road could be followed to world-class Olympic swimming. The avenue that you chose would take you toward wherever your interest would lead you—depending on how hard you were willing to work, your focus, determination, and passion, as well as your God-given talents and natural abilities.

At every stage, the coaches and administrators emphasized that each one of those roads was as worthy as the other. We knew that, without question. We also knew that at some level and at some point, Olympic aspirations came into play for most NBAC swimmers and their parents. To combat the habits of crazy swim moms and dads who obsessed over their children's times, micromanaging their records and rankings on index cards, we were reminded of the sobering reality that the chances of making the Olympic team—which was chosen only every four years—was something like .0002 percent. (The official national swim organization, USA Swimming uses that statistic to point out that there are approximately 250,000 competitive swimmers vying for fifty-two spots on the U.S. Olympic team.)

Once we had the practice calendar down, we were soon exposed to the grueling competition schedule that was like a minefield of meets all along the way. There were state meets, zones, followed by competitive levels that included juniors, seniors, the national B team, the national A team, Olympic trials, World Championships, the Olympic Games. Like most of the public, we had never heard of most of these competitions or teams, for that matter, but we would start hearing about them more and more.

Just as our children were learning the all-important adage that records are made to be broken, we were taught that the world record breaking often took place at such venues as the World Championships that were held in the years before and after the Olympics, as well as at international meets like the Pan Pacifics and the Pan American Games.

Early in our competitive experiences, I had the chance to witness some of the excesses of swim parents. I couldn't stand hearing them berate or humiliate their children any more than I could stand it from the parents of my students at school. Yes, I did get crazy briefly in our early days, keeping the index cards on all the races for both girls—until that became much too time-consuming. Thank goodness! After that I was able to relax and enjoy watching the girls swim—and cheering for them loudly from the sidelines or the stands.

Whether at the meets or at practice, Michael was also watching his sisters. From the time that he was a toddler, when I would scoop him out of the minivan in his royal blue blanket sleeper and then let him toddle around inside, he was paying attention. It is no exaggeration to say that he was given a head start, an early education in swimming when he was between the ages of two and six, sponging up so much knowledge from watching Hilary and Whitney. At meets when we arrived before 7:00 a.m. and often didn't leave until after noon, he was there for hours at a stretch. Sometimes he was playing in the stands or in a large nearby gymnasium or activity room with siblings of other swimmers. But even then, he never missed a beat. Years later, I was surprised at how much he had been observing and studying the whole time. When he hit his first races, it was incredible to see him take off like a bullet, with perfect execution. It was almost as if he had been developing his skills mentally in advance of actually trying things out.

I'd already seen this with Whitney to a certain extent. The first time I saw her compete—in freestyle and in a short-course race—I watched a metamorphosis from the second she bent her legs to prepare to dive. In that stance, I saw what a compact little powerhouse she was, with a look of eagle-eyed determination that was a beautiful sight to behold. The next thing I knew she was off the blocks faster than I'd ever seen her—as if catapulted into the water by a slingshot. As though effortlessly, she flew to the other side of the pool and touched first.

Whitney had been watching Hilary and improving on her game all the while. And I suspect the lessons were from not only the wins but also the challenges. One of the bravest moments I can recall from Hilary's childhood was when she was nine, still at RASAC, and we were at one of her meets in Aberdeen, not too far from Havre de Grace. At the last minute, one of the coaches assigned her to an empty lane that had opened up in the 1500 freestyle after one of the swimmers scratched.

This wasn't an age group race; it was called an open/even, which meant she would be pitted against eighteen-year-olds like Brandy Wood and Heather Ray—top swimmers. Distraught, in tears, she knew this was like swimming hara-kiri. But Hilary didn't back down. And the coach gave her lots of credit, walking right alongside her, encouraging her, urging her on, and helping her sync into her rhythm to swim the distance. Hilary was the last swimmer to reach the wall, but as she swam her final strokes, all the older girls stayed in the pool—cheering at the top of their lungs and congratulating her for finishing the race. An early DP moment! And that was before they were called DP moments.

Some of the peculiarities of the swim game, we were all to learn, sometimes came down to the luck of the draw—things we couldn't control, like when your birthday happened to fall. Usually you weren't being thrown in to swim against eighteen-year-olds; you swam in an age group bracket. Starting with eight years old and under, you then advanced to the nine- and ten-year-old bracket, then eleven/twelve, thirteen/fourteen, and fifteen/sixteen. Logically, you did best when you were swimming in the upper end of your age group. Since zones were in March before her birthday, Hilary was fine if she was at the upper end of her age group: if she was ten, she would be swimming against nine-year-olds and younger tens too. But she would be at the lower end when it came time to go to the next age group; for example, when she had just turned eleven, she was swimming against more experienced eleven- and twelve-year-olds. Whitney and Michael both had better "swimming birthdays," because when competing in age group competitions, they were both swimming at the top of their age, and because they both advanced out of their age group faster. But in Hilary's case, her birthday was akin to Russian roulette. We never knew where the cutoff dates would fall and what the competition was going to be. To toughen yourself up, as swimmer or parent, you had to become basically fatalistic and accept that the outcome was going to be in the cards.

Once Whitney started accelerating out of her age group, it was inevitable that she would eventually have to swim against Hilary. For a while, we avoided it, thankfully. But the day arrived when the two happened to be seeded next to each other in the same heat—the 100-yard butterfly.

Barely able to watch, I kept thinking, *Oh, dear, how can this be?* As soon as the race started, the Phelps sisters shot out into the pool, neck and neck, unaware that seconds later the race was called off because of a false start from one of the other swimmers. Hilary and Whitney just charged through the water, swimming a full 25 yards, flipping at the wall, and getting almost all the way back before they could be stopped.

That's how intense they were! No one remembers who won that race.

Almost everyone we encountered at NBAC, including the parents, had a certain intensity. Some of us used to laugh that becoming a part of this inner circle of parents was like signing your soul over to the devil! It also meant you were going to pay your dues literally and figuratively, chaperoning trips, volunteering, and mentoring other parents. If you were one of the inner circle of the parents who were among the most active and involved with the club, it was expected that you would bring others into the fold as well, make them feel welcome and loved, and encourage them to keep the parking-lot chatter down.

It wasn't so much about the noise and the congestion that occurred out there with the gossip among disgruntled or busybody parents who were prone to that kind of talk. Keeping the parking-lot chatter down was much more about maintaining the professionalism and team spirit that were central to the NBAC way.

That made sense to me because I honestly didn't have time. Whenever one of my kids wasn't practicing, we went out to a nearby fast-food place where they could do their homework (and I could do mine) in a quiet, well-lit spot. Sometimes we would use the time to go grocery shopping. I wanted to avoid that parking-lot gossip, to help out and do what was expected of me, and maintain the same level of decorum that elite swimmers ought to have. That attitude earned me respect and standing for my children too. Of course, they earned that respect as well by their own leadership and strong work ethic. Unlike some parents, I didn't pack their bags or help carry them, nor did I oversee how they handled their gear. I wanted them to be self-sufficient and to get the most out of their pastime and their passion.

Like every parent, in the earlier years I had no idea how far the swimming thing would go. Anything could happen, I assumed. But in the meantime, I was sure that swimming was teaching my kids many lasting life skills.

Like every sport that has its own language, culture, and insider's knowledge, swimming—we learned at the start—involves a level of courtesy and respect that is expected of all participants. Children are taught to refer to their coaches and instructors not by first names alone but with a Miss, Ms., Mrs., Mr., or Coach in front of their given names. Cathy Lears, a great friend and fellow swim mom, as well as an instructor who had literally grown up swimming at Meadowbrook, would always be "Ms. Cathy" to my three kids—even though Michael was the only one who actually took swim lessons from her. (Actually, Michael was the only Phelps to take lessons, at least at what would be classified a competitive swim school as offered by NBAC.)

From the moment I met Cathy, I felt that our paths were destined to cross. Somehow we got to talking one day and I happened to mention how Fred and I had attended Fairmont State, where I'd been the president of my sorority.

"I was president of my sorority too." Cathy laughed. I had found a kindred spirit who enjoyed taking charge and tended toward perfectionism as I did.

"Really, which sorority?"

"Phi Mu."

What a small world! When I told her that I'd been a Phi Mu, we learned next that we had both attended the national Phi Mu fraternity conference in New Orleans the same year, when we were seniors and graduated from college.

From then on, thanks to Cathy and everyone who welcomed us into the fold, NBAC really did become our extended family. For the most part, I assumed that Fred felt the same. He wasn't on-site as much during practice sessions when they conflicted with his night shift schedule, but he stayed involved as a timekeeper and later as a stroke and turn judge who officiated during meets, also assisting with the setting up, breaking down, and storing of the equipment. Officiating in his capacity entailed studying swimming manuals and protocol, as well as passing a test measuring knowledge of the sport. Timing and officiating weren't for me, but I found my calling in the hospitality rooms that parents helped run during meets.

On the weekends or on evenings sometimes when lanes were available, some of the other moms and I would swim too, taking out the kick boards and paddling along, more for social enjoyment than serious exercise. It reminded me of my teen years growing up in Westernport, where the community pool in the summer was where you went to look beautiful in your bikini and get a suntan—a far cry from competitive swimming.

It didn't take long in our journey with NBAC for me to make a life-altering discovery: there are only so many hours in the day! Where once I had sought to defy time and squeeze everything and more into twenty-four hours, I finally had to establish some priorities. Some of the extras just had to go. No more being a Brownies leader, no more teaching Sunday school. Even making it to Sunday church services wasn't easy. Rather than beat myself up about it, I took solace in the idea that spending Sundays at the pool was a way of showing reverence and love for life.

We eventually acknowledged that the pool was our church. It was all inclusive. You didn't have to believe in God, say a prayer, or worship in a church, synagogue, or temple. You could simply embrace the belief that God was with us everywhere we went.

Sometimes, on quiet Sunday mornings with just the sounds of water being moved through by solitary swimmers, giving me the gift of time to search my soul and know what I was really feeling about where we were headed—or not—as a family, it really felt a lot like church.

For most of the years between 1987 and 1991, I did a terrific job of reassuring myself that everything was going to be fine between me and Fred. But deep down, I wasn't so sure. Some of our issues were concerns I knew many couples faced at different stages. Our romantic life wasn't helped by the fact that he worked the night swing shift and I worked during the day. Positive communication was not easy when we were rarely home at the same time. Yet whenever I made a suggestion about moving closer into Baltimore so we could cut down on the driving time—bringing up my argument that a big dream house out in the country wasn't worth it when we were there only to sleep—Fred was wary. He enjoyed living in the country, out in rural America. Over time, he became resentful if I even brought up the subject.

After a while, I felt the same. Finally, begrudgingly, Fred gave in and we moved to a neighborhood five minutes from the pool at Loyola. Five minutes! It was a beautiful redbrick Colonial-style house in a charming Baltimore County neighborhood on a tree-lined street. With Michael now six years old, Whitney eleven, and Hilary thirteen, it was such a relief to have the family consolidated—closer to schools and pools—with an open door policy for their friends and swimming buddies to congregate at our place. I was so happy about the move that the morning and afternoon commute to Harford County, where I was still teaching, was a small price to pay.

Even as we settled into city living, Fred never warmed up to this move. He missed the quiet, the country living, the distance from neighbors. He worried about higher house payments, property taxes, and the higher cost of living in Baltimore County—on top of the swimming fees that definitely added up the more involved we became. On top of the dues for membership, more competitions meant more entry fees, on top of travel expenses like hotels and food. Later at the national and international levels, the swim associations helped defray some costs for the swimmers—but not all.

Not long after the move, I began to sense that there was a growing distance between Fred and me that, try as I might, wasn't something that I could fix. While I had certainly learned that marriage, like life, is never as simple or perfect as I'd once imagined, it was still tough for me to accept that there might not be a ready-made solution. After all, I was an educator, a problem solver by nature and training. Yet complicated matters of the heart aren't so easily identified and confronted in such matter-of-fact ways. My only solution was to hope that once we moved past the initial adjustment period to the new home and new routine, we would return to our former balance.

Then again, it didn't take much for old insecurities and trust issues to creep back in. This was the case when Fred announced he was taking a second job with a local private-security detail as a law enforcement agent. Since he had taken on the extra work to help make ends meet with the added expenses, I loved his willingness to provide for the family. But the less we saw of each other, the wider the gulf was between us. When he didn't come home at the appointed times, I started to wonder if what had happened before was happening again.

And sure enough it did. With our previous separation, I had convinced myself that I could control whether he came back or not. By this stage, I knew that it wasn't in my hands.

The moment when it hit me that the gulf between us was too wide to be bridged was the beginning of the end of our marriage. It wasn't the end of our family or the role Fred played and would continue to play as my children's father. It was nonetheless very sad. But even so, I wasn't going to stop to mourn. I knew I needed to be strong.

SEVEN

Just a Normal Family

The best way to describe the next five roller-coaster years that led us up to the 1996 Olympic trials is to quote Charles Dickens's first line from *A Tale of Two Cities*, "It was the best of times, it was the worst of times."

There were some major high points and meaningful breakthroughs, just as there were some devastating lows. And yet, for all the ups and downs, I made up my mind early on that we were going to get through them, even though sometimes I honestly didn't always know how. I just knew we could and we would. Whatever was going to happen, my most important goal was for us to make it through together as a normal family.

Maybe that was an unrealistic goal. Especially with the unofficial standoff between Fred and me. We had not come to a decision to separate, although he moved into the den, which was actually the garage that we had remodeled and turned into a wing of its own. We were aloof in our communication, though not angry. Sometimes I even wondered it he wanted me to be more confrontational, to yell or throw a fit.

Maybe it was the way my mother raised me, but throwing fits wasn't in my nature. And anger wouldn't help me to understand what had happened. I'd heard that in midlife crises men sometimes felt envious of the attention their children received from their wives and needed to be the center of attention again just as when the couple were newlyweds. I'd heard that one of the reasons some men step out of marriages was to find that attention or adoration elsewhere. Could that be it? I went over and over it in my mind. Who even knew?

In those years I was starting to wrap up the very long but rewarding process of obtaining my master's degree (to be completed in 1998 at Loyola College) in education and supervision—the career path I ultimately wanted to pursue. Even though it was not yet in the foreseeable future, I decided in those days that if I ever did seek my doctorate, I would write my dissertation on the family structure of individuals in law enforcement and the drowning of the family in their lives. I'm not saying that all our issues had to do with work stress and the cynicism and hopelessness of what he was dealing with day to day on the job. But the man who was sitting in the den just zoned out watching television seemed so different from the gallant fellow with the flair for drama who had made such a production of the arrival of our babies that each time we went to the hospital, he managed to smash his Stetson hat.

For the first time I had to face the reality that I didn't have a ready-made solution. Having gone through a separation before, I felt even less inclined to talk to others about what was happening this time. Even though I didn't share what was going on with my mother or my siblings, as I might have in the past, I thought a lot about what Mom must have gone through when she was newly widowed—about those couple of years when she first needed to find her footing. And then I thought about how she threw herself into her work as a teaching assistant and managed to support herself and my two younger siblings on so little. Throughout that time, she never ceased being a rock of support and source of caring counsel to all four of us. Never once did she lose her vivacious, joyous love of learning and life.

Mom's example was an inspiration in this dark time and a steadying force as I watched my old storybook vision for our marriage fade away. I couldn't deny that the "home sweet home" that lived in my dreams wasn't turning out the way that it was supposed to be. No, I wasn't going to fix it or stitch it back together. Nor was I going to play the blame game.

Whatever I was going to do, I first had to think about it deeply, pray about it, digest it, and then do what I needed to do so that I could learn from it.

Was I ready to be a single mom? No, but then who is? Just from a financial standpoint, that was a very scary proposition. A single mom of three growing children—on a schoolteacher's salary? Of course, I knew Fred would contribute to our financial well-being (and he did). I also was aware that, as it was, we were already very stretched supporting one household on two salaries; it would get much tougher with two households, not to mention that we were living in an upper-middle-class neighborhood with a cost of living that was rising in the boom years of the 1990s.

Clearly, as a home economics teacher for twenty years at three middle schools with a wide-ranging student population in terms of family income, I'd learned a lot about practical considerations for single-parent households and other challenges in helping my students meet their needs. That was why I focused on life skills for self-sufficiency when it came to cooking, teaching such practices as the basics of microwave operation and the preparation of nutritious meals on a tight budget.

The issue of money had also been on my mind when we were shopping for Hilary and Whitney's first major trip for a meet in Atlanta. We had splurged on new outfits from the Limited, which all the girls on the team had to have. You could say it was a tradition to buy something special for a trip of this importance. They were so excited about this invitational meet out of town and the fact that they were going to be traveling on an airplane to a big city, without their parents, to compete on an elite age-group, national level. The outfits were part of it!

That moment had coincided, by the way, with the first time I could ever remember my mother criticizing me. I was crushed. Me, the daughter who always wanted to please her parents, was being told by my mother that she didn't approve of one of my decisions.

Leoma Davisson put it this way: "I don't believe that you are sending your two girls to Atlanta with people you don't know."

"Well, I trust them and there are multiple chaperones per age group—both males and females. This is the number one swim team in Maryland as well as the number one age-group swim team in the country, and these are people I've met and can trust."

I had to remind myself that the farthest from western Maryland that my mother had ever been was New York City. Not a hop, skip, and jump, to use her term, but she wasn't a world traveler. I also had to remember the time that she and Dad took me to Dulles Airport so I could fly to California to a youth conference for the Future Homemakers of America conference and they both cried!

The good news was that Hilary and Whitney came home with rave reports about what a wonderful time they had had at the meet and how staying in a hotel was so much fun; all in all, it was a fantastic learning experience. From their coaches, I heard that they both swam well, each asserting themselves as elite swimmers with more achievements to come.

Still, I was sensitive to Mom's comments. They might not have made me feel so hurt if they hadn't come right around the time when I was trying to figure out how to deal with the impasse in my marriage. I have to admit that part of what weighed on me was the stigma associated with divorce. Maybe that was the prim and proper "English" side of me, as my mom always said, but I could remember when I was growing up that a divorcée was considered to be almost a fallen woman. But mainly I was concerned for my daughters and my son, who needed their father in their lives.

On certain days, I would resolve to hang in there until the three graduated from high school, to keep the family intact and under the same roof. On other days, it made no sense to me to keep the family intact if Fred was going to be just sitting in the den. Besides, at this point, I had friends of the children coming in and out all day, every day. "Let's go to Miss Debbie's house" was a constant refrain I loved hearing. The last thing I wanted was to have to say no or keep the den off limits.

The situation was untenable. But answers were slow in coming.

Our saving grace throughout this time was swimming. The rigors of NBAC, demanding as they were, were a godsend. We never missed practice. That would be like cutting off your fingers! Such was the level of our commitment and the priority we as a family placed on swimming. Ironically, for a second there, I wasn't sure that Michael was going to go for it with the same passion as his sisters. Or at all! Just as Whitney had been intimidated by the 50-meter pool at Meadowbrook the first time she saw it, when seven-year-old Michael officially started lessons with Cathy Lears, he was somewhat resistant. Apparently, what he said those first few times was that he didn't want to get wet!

That didn't last long, needless to say. The real challenge once he was in the pool turned out to be that he wasn't too fond of putting his face in the water. In hindsight, this makes more sense to me than it did at the time. After all, Michael was a keen observer who was constantly watching everything and everyone, often without our realizing how much he was picking up. So maybe his resistance to submerging his face in the water was about not wanting to give up his powers of sight. Years later, when he would have a couple of close calls over goggle malfunctions, I would flash on the past and realize how disorienting that experience could be.

In the meantime, however, Miss Cathy found the perfect solution by first teaching Michael to swim on his back and then easing him into swimming on his stomach. Everything clicked. Somehow he used the fear of not being able to see to do the opposite—to be able to "see" in the water with all his senses. It was almost uncanny how early on he began to experience what Whitney also exhibited—a *feel* for the water.

This is perhaps not so different from how any well-tuned athlete has a feel for his or her arena. That feel for the water was one of the differences between the three Phelps siblings. Whitney and Michael, who were raised exclusively as swimmers at NBAC, talked about having it. Hilary, a no less passionate swimmer and competitor, didn't talk about the feel of the water the same way, or at least not until she was about to enter college. Later on, whenever both Whitney and Michael went to meets, they would jump into the pool and get a feel for the water. There was no science to this, no evaluation for a particular buoyancy or special quality they were looking for. But that first feel was always an indication of how they were going to swim at that meet or competition.

One way Whitney psyched herself into maintaining stamina with some of the most grueling practice sets that I'd ever seen for thirteen- and fourteen-year-olds was to focus on the feel of the water—her love for how it felt. Later, Michael would actually call on the phone to tell me how he loved a certain pool. A month before the Olympic trials in 2008 in Omaha at the new pool at the Qwest Center, Michael went there for a pre-Olympic meet and reported back, "I love this pool, Mom, I just love it!" Feeling comfortable in the water was important for Michael, who thrives when his comfort level is high. And if he liked the feel of the water in Omaha, we had only to wait to see how he would feel about the water at the Water Cube in Beijing.

But back when he was in the third grade and only learning to feel the water, those days were way out in the clouds. I do recall, however, that it was in that era when a few of the NBAC parents, as well as parents throughout the state of Maryland, began making comments at age-group meets about Michael. Most of their observations were just the kinds of comments all parents make as a way of being supportive about one another's children, so I didn't put much stock in them. Nonetheless I remember certain instances when we'd be sitting there and as he raced right by, charging down a lane full steam, people would take notice and even say to one another, "Wow! Did you see that? He's fast!"

I didn't think much about it since that's how he was out of the water too—always zooming by, off to do something that appeared to be exciting and fun or off to investigate something of great interest.

In some of the previous school years and in subsequent ones, I heard a range of comments from Michael's teachers about issues that later led to a diagnosis of ADHD (attention deficit/hyperactivity disorder). The comments were as mild as "Michael has a hard time sitting still," to "Michael doesn't show much of an interest in reading" or "He needs to take more time with writing," to "His inability to focus and maintain attention is disruptive to the classroom and there is a possibility that difficulties will lie ahead of you."

In as diplomatic a way as possible, I would confront some of those teachers who questioned his capacity for learning and tell them point-blank, "You're wrong." For one thing, I knew as a teacher that all children deserve our belief and our willingness to help them learn and be successful. For another, I knew that children learn differently from one another. So I was none too pleased by such dismissive remarks—about my child or anyone's child. And I also knew Michael and had observed how his learning process was much faster, like that of other students, when he was engaged and interested. Again, he could absorb massive amounts of information, process it, distill it, and then understand, but he still needed to be taught the skills to express what he had learned. In my estimation, teachers who said he couldn't learn weren't doing their job of accommodating the different learning styles of all their students.

There was a memorable incident when Michael was in elementary school and came home with an audiotape recorded in class of the teacher reading with each of the students. I listened as the teacher was starting to have Michael read but then said "Excuse me," as Michael let out a big sigh before she turned off the tape. Then it came on again and he seemed discouraged and frustrated by the interruption but didn't give up.

After we listened to the tape together, I asked Michael, "Why did the teacher stop recording before you read to her?"

"Oh," he explained, "someone was acting up when it was my turn to read and she had to tell him to stop and that took time away from me."

The fact that he didn't complain or give up showed me his determination as well as his sensitivity at being let down by his teacher. He had the feeling of being let down a lot in school, I think. And that wasn't fair.

Later, not long before he was tested and given a diagnosis of

ADHD along with a prescription for medication—which he would take for two years between the ages of nine and eleven—I would come to an understanding as to how the swimming pool was the best possible classroom for Michael. And I also had my say with a few of the teachers who complained about his inability to sit still and keep his attention and focus.

I'd long avoided throwing in my two cents about how my children's teachers ought to be teaching. And I certainly didn't like it when parents told me how to do my job. I wasn't going to do that with Michael's teachers, but I also wasn't about to keep my mouth entirely shut. So when they said he had trouble focusing, I said, "You haven't seen him sitting at a meet for four hours, waiting for his turn to swim. Don't tell me he can't focus; he can." Did I add that maybe their classroom experience was boring the students to death? No. But I did say at a swim meet you arrived at the crack of dawn, sat there for half a day to compete, often for less than two minutes or slightly more, maybe five minutes, and if that wasn't sitting still in hyperfocus, I didn't know what was. And I also suggested that in my experience, when learning is meaningful and authentic, a child will sit forever.

This isn't to say that I was upset by the ADHD diagnosis. I often provide support and guidance to parents with suggestions to consider when dealing with what can be a stigma or a label that worries them. First, it's important to avoid going down an alarmist path. Second, I recommend being open to using different resources—the school, medical professionals such as your pediatrician, the literature that is amply available, and other parents. It turned out that what Michael needed most was structure. We already had swimming, but it could have been other sports, arts, or any structured activity in which he could be successful—not on his own but with guidance and support to attain consistency, time on task, and a feeling of fun and fulfillment. For anyone looking for that structure, it may take some trial and error to find the right fit, but those elements are key.

I also wasn't resistant to trying the medication recommended by our physician. However, it didn't go over well with Fred, who resisted the idea that his son might need medication. My feeling, having taught students who were on medication for ADHD, was that it could help. Besides, we weren't in the classroom with him all day, so if it could help him become a better learner and be even more successful in school, why wouldn't we try?

We eventually went with the advice of our medical professionals, and the medication definitely helped. After two years, Michael was the one who opted to wean himself off it and was given our doctor's okay—at a time when, remarkably, he was making As and Bs in middle school, was playing four sports all extraordinarily well, and, unbeknownst to us, was about to take a major leap in the pool.

One of the discoveries we made while helping Michael with homework for subjects like English composition was that the best way for him to understand abstract problems was to convert them into real world examples. When he did this, he was a whiz! He was already strong in math, but if a problem could be expressed in terms of swim times or swimming pools, he could practically do calculus in his head. If he was free to use his rich visual imagination to come up with stories to write, he could give those compositions a beginning, middle, and end—just like a swimming race has a beginning, middle, and end. Later on, when we'd exhausted my expertise at math, I knew it was time to bring in a tutor and, what do you know, as it so happened, one of the summer coaches from Meadowbrook, Chris Conaway, fit the bill.

When Michael was eight years old, those issues were not yet upon us, but one of the most positive influences in his early education was a part of his life. Barbara Kines, his third-grade teacher, was one of those amazing educators who plant seeds of possibilities and belief in students that last forever. Mrs. Kines was an extraordinary teacher not only because she saw all of Michael's potential, but because she saw the potential of each and every student. She cared about every child in that classroom and knew how every child learned, what made every child tick.

As far as I know, Barbara Kines wasn't aware of what was happening behind the scenes in our household that year. Perhaps she was sensitive enough to know that the added nurturing she gave to every student was important at that time or that Michael could use the sense of stability he gained from her classroom. Yet for me it was what she did outside the schoolhouse that was so amazing. At many of Michael's swim meets, I'd look up and there she would be with her husband, Roger, sitting in the stands to cheer Michael on. Mrs. Kines did that for all her students, attending their baseball games, dance performances, and music recitals. That's how much she loved them and included them as part of her extended family.

It was all the more meaningful that Mr. Roger came with her to these events when we learned that he was legally blind. One time at a meet after Michael's race, Mr. Roger congratulated him on a great job. He said that Michael should keep it up, just like he had done that day.

I remember the quizzical look on Michael's face as he thought about the fact that Roger couldn't actually see him. Michael said, "I don't mean to be disrespectful, but how could you tell how I swam?"

Roger smiled and explained, "I could hear the crowd cheering for you. I could hear you in the water." Roger Kines had his own way of using his senses to feel what was happening. He felt something that day about Michael's abilities that maybe I didn't even know about yet. Indeed, I stayed in touch with Barbara over the coming years, and she told me she'd seen something in Michael too.

Part of my training as a swim parent at NBAC was not to put too much stock into positive or negative predictions and not to get ahead of the game. That's what I attempted to do with all the swim action going on for both Hilary and Whitney.

After Hilary set the thirteen/fourteen NBAC age-group record in the 1500-meter freestyle (a record that held for many years)—a pinnacle in her early career—I was stunned that next Christmas when I drove her home from practice and she started sobbing when we pulled into our driveway, collapsing in my arms and telling me, "I just can't do this anymore."

Hilary was a coach's dream, a classic overachiever, always pushing herself, never complaining. Her coach Tom noticed how she used her mental strengths in the pool, an indication of her great potential, and the bar was set high. Because she had moved so fast initially, Hilary later recalled that she was never able to steep herself in the fundamentals of the sport. She also would say that it wasn't until she went to the University of Richmond to swim collegiately that many of the lessons that Murray Stephens and the coaches at NBAC had tried to teach her finally clicked.

Then again, I will always remember the moment when Murray Stephens acknowledged Hilary for her talent and hard work—not so much by what he said but by his actions. Hilary was attempting to make her senior national cut in order to attend the U.S. Senior National meet the following season. When she didn't make it, I remember him sitting down next to her poolside and cupping her chin in his hands, sending the message for her to "keep her chin up," to never give up. That was a very powerful way of letting a young teenage girl find her balance between swimming and life.

Balance was always key to Hilary's well-being. And that's what we were able to talk about in the car that morning. My approach was to listen, ask questions, introduce some common sense, and try to come at the situation logically, calmly. After talking about it, Hilary said she didn't want to quit swimming and that she could handle the demands. Her solution was to find the balance by slowing down her pace and cutting herself some slack.

"Absolutely," I agreed. Well, other issues would come up later when her social life became more active. But all in all, I thought Hilary's balancing act was healthy—especially with the instability in the house with her father there but not there.

Our talk was also an opportunity for me to acknowledge her academic achievements. In fact, a couple of years earlier, when we were still living in Harford County, I was able to arrange a boundary transfer for Hilary to attend Southampton Middle School, where I'd been teaching all this time, in the Bel Air area. Since she had swim practice at 4:00 p.m., we could leave school right at the bell on the days when the carpool could pick up the younger two, and make our way down the Beltway to Baltimore. Thanks to the luck of the draw, she ended up in my sixth-grade home economics class and I was able to observe her in the classroom as a student.

I knew of course that she was a straight A student, but now I was able to see firsthand how gifted, talented, and smart she was in school. Every parent should have the opportunity to observe their middle school child in the classroom. Hilary, to her credit, was very conscientious about setting aside our mother/daughter relationship in the classroom. She always raised her hand politely and referred to me as Mrs. Phelps—except for one time when she wanted my attention and said, "Oh, Mom . . ." before she caught herself.

In the course of our talk while parked in the driveway that day, Hilary needed to hear that I was proud of her. Wise as she was, she perceived that I needed to hear those words too. "I'm so proud of you, Mom," she began.

"Really?"

"Teacher of the year!" she reminded me.

Hilary was right. I had a victory to celebrate—the fact that I'd been named Maryland Family and Consumer Science Teacher of the Year in that period, the first of two times that I would be honored with that award.

From tears to cheers, our talk that winter morning meant the world to me—more than I think Hilary knew. In any case, in the months that followed, she was the epitome of resilience and inspired me in the process.

I didn't hear another concern about swimming until her junior year in high school, when she came home and said, in a sincere tone that suggested that she'd given the matter a lot of thought, "Mom, I really want to play lacrosse."

Now, I was not too fond of this idea for a few reasons. But knowing her as I do, I needed to ask questions rather than say nay or yay. "Hilary," I began, knowing the answer but asking it anyway, "have you ever played lacrosse before? Have you ever held a lacrosse stick in your hand?"

"No, I haven't. But I think I'd pick it up quickly."

"Right. Although . . . how do you think you're going to do, playing against girls who have played lacrosse all through high school?"

"I don't know, but I want to play lacrosse."

Then came the clincher when I reminded her of her goal of swimming at the college level. I went on, "You have one more year until you graduate. I want to make sure you are willing to throw away all the years invested in swimming and the possibility of a scholarship so you can play lacrosse. What do you think?"

She sighed and laughed. Those questions were all Hilary needed to say good-bye to her passing fancy for lacrosse.

Unlike her sister, Whitney never expressed resistance or ambivalence toward swimming, at least not to me. As early as 1992, right around the time that she turned twelve, I watched her turn on her powerjets and raise her game with every practice and every meet. Whitney always took what she was asked to do by her coaches and then delivered three notches higher.

Before she was about to compete in zones, I was told that Whitney had a chance to advance to junior nationals and wouldn't be swimming zones at all. Everyone at NBAC and in the Maryland swimming community assumed that meant I would step down from the position of team manager, which involved traveling with the team to zone meets. But I stayed on anyway for the next two years to oversee zones for seventy-five or more swimmers—handling their hotel reservations and meals, organizing special team wear and travel apparel, you name it! Some of the parents were surprised that I would be team manager without any Phelps offspring at those meets. For me, it was all about adding the mom touch for the other children too and about having fun myself. That was my opportunity to prove that parents could also use a reminder that there is no *I* in the word *team*.

At one of the zone meets that took place over Easter weekend in Princeton, New Jersey, I was planning my Easter baskets for Hilary, Whitney, and Michael when it occurred to me that the Maryland swimmers who were traveling out of town would be missing their family celebration. I decided at that moment to have Easter baskets prepared and shipped all the way to Princeton. With the help of cooperative coconspirators who were parents from across the state (Coach Tom Hines pitched in too), the baskets were labeled with the swimmers' names and then hidden around the hotel parking lot on Easter morning. Before boarding the bus, we had a joyful scene as the swimmers, who were still a little sleepy, came out before sunrise and had a free-for-all as they each found their own basket.

You don't have to believe in the Easter Bunny to appreciate the treats of the season. Feel free to borrow ideas from this example of the zones basket full of treats, edible and nonedible, that you can tailor for nonswimmers too, no matter how old the recipient:

Dyed eggs—with vintage decals! Red, gold, black, and white jelly beans (Maryland colors!), assorted Peeps, a chocolate bunny or two, chocolate-covered marshmallow eggs, pastel M&M's, swim magazines, travel toiletries, water bottles, sports bars, and school supplies too!

So, while I continued my stint as team mom for zones, Whitney, age twelve, having made the U.S. Junior team, continued her ascent in the pool and traveled to Paris for her first international meet—accompanied by coaches from throughout the country and by paid chaperones who work for the U.S. swim association. At higher levels of competition, parent volunteers were not brought on as chaperones but were certainly encouraged to attend as spectators. Fred was able to attend this first international meet to watch Whitney swim. For Whitney it was her first opportunity to see how she would handle the pressure of competing against swimmers from around the world. The reports from everyone when they returned home were that she had been incredibly poised and confident in her events.

The following year she returned to Paris for her second international meet, asserting herself in the 200-meter butterfly. The only asterisk to that trip was that she slipped and fell on the starting blocks, causing pain to her back but not putting a dent in her determination. The result, a year later, was that at the age of fourteen she won the national championship for the 200-meter butterfly, qualifying next for World Championships in Rome, Italy. Whitney placed ninth in her main event, a coup at this level of competition that increased her chances of being a contender for the 1996 Olympic Games—two years away.

As a nine-year-old starting to turn a few more heads with his own races, Michael diligently followed both Hilary's and Whitney's successes. He prided himself in knowing their swim times and records, along with most of the competitive swimmers in his age group and older, and could have told anyone that at this time both his sisters were in the top ten nationally. He could have also told anyone that by the time Olympic trials were to be scheduled, Whitney would be ranked third in the world in the 200-meter butterfly and first in the United States.

As exciting as all these developments were, behind the scenes the tension in our household was taking a toll on all of us. We all kept up a brave, positive, normal front, but as I later learned, I was not the only one of us who was hurting badly inside.

Our pediatrician had once remarked that all three of my children had an unusually high level of tolerance to pain. This was said in reference to their frequent ear infections. Maybe this tolerance of theirs led me to take longer than it should have to realize that keeping my marriage going for their benefit was doing none of us any good.

Later, in her first year at the University of Richmond, where Hilary was awarded a full athletic scholarship and went on to swim all four years, she would write about how emotionally challenging this time was for her. It broke my heart to read how she had carried a feeling of responsibility on her shoulders:

My family is what American society classifies as a "normal" family. I have two parents, a mother and a father and a sister and a brother. Everyone is very supportive of one another and for the most part, everyone gets along very well. . . . At first, when the whole separation with my parents was going through, I thought that it was my fault. We had moved into the city so that I could swim, my mom was devoting a lot of time to the swim club, and my dad didn't like it. This caused a lot of problems with my parents. It was especially hard for Michael, my little brother. . . . It was really hard on the whole family. There were times when I couldn't do my homework, or I would have to get out of practice. My friends were very supportive and my parents tried to be. They told us that this kind of thing happens all the time. I realized that it did, that wasn't the problem. It just wasn't supposed to happen to me.

At the time, I didn't know how much all three of my children were internalizing their feelings. But once I did begin to pick up on their pain, I realized that I wasn't preventing it by pretending to be strong and stoic. It dawned on me that whether or not this was normal, it was happening to us. It finally sank in.

It also hit me at last that Fred was going to keep on living in the den unless I did something. That's when I called someone I knew who referred me to a lawyer. The moment he answered the phone, I felt stronger than I had in quite some time. It was like having a wave of relief wash over me. I asked him if he would meet me that evening, and before I knew it, we were wrapping up our meeting and he had agreed to help draw up separation/divorce papers.

Remember the parking-lot gossip? The news spread quickly. Everyone was shocked. The more vocal among them said, "You're not really going to do this, are you?" (The funny thing is that those who raised their eyebrows the most ended up divorced within ten years. I suppose that made me the pioneer!)

I didn't explain, complain, or blame. Basically, I let them know that I had realized that I could not live like this. I cared about my family and had finally accepted that Fred and I had stopped growing together and, indeed, had grown apart. This was not going to break me. It would be hard, but it wasn't the end of the world.

In the meantime I made sure I could pay the cost of various swim fees on credit—payments over time—knowing there might be lean years up ahead. I will never forget the generosity and support I was given at that time. It was all I needed to be able to tell Fred that papers were being drawn up.

He agreed to everything. We shared custody but I had the children 24-7, and he committed to financial support. And true to his word, he wouldn't let us down. Even so, it was going to be a struggle for us. But what mattered most is that our children understood that we both still loved each of them as we always had. I committed to doing everything humanly possible to make sure Fred and his children had contact. After they turned eighteen, though, that responsibility would be between him and them.

With that, he packed the last of his things and moved out for good.

In anticipation of single parenthood, I knew it was high time I got a job in Baltimore County. Logistically it was the only thing to do as well as an exciting opportunity to move my career to the next place. For several months I had been putting feelers out and had learned of no openings until finally someone alerted me to a position at Southwest Academy, a Baltimore County magnet school, that Darryl Bonds, an ex-marine, had been hired to help turn around as the principal. Without knowing anyone at the school, I called and arranged for an interview.

Before the appointed day arrived, I happened to receive a phone call from a friend of the family in the Tri-Towns that one of Fred's aunts had passed away. Since I had a free afternoon, I decided the right thing to do was to go and pay my respects. Michael, now in the fourth grade, was able to come with me after practice—giving us a couple of hours to make the drive together and talk and check in with each other.

When we arrived at the funeral home in the Tri-Towns, no one was there. So, with no reason to stay for very long, I signed the registrar and headed back home to Baltimore. On the way, instead of talking about all kinds of serious subjects like grades and swimming, the two of us were just cracking up, singing loud to songs on the radio, and having fun. Now, Michael may tell this story differently and choose to say I'm not the greatest driver. Or that I'm too slow or overcautious. But I'm a great driver! I have a near perfect record! It's just that this day, I was eager to get home and track down the girls, and we were having such a blast together, I happened to be speeding and a state trooper pulled me over. Sirens going and lights flashing!

As I moved over to the shoulder, Michael reached over the seat to grab my license out of my pocketbook as I pulled the registration from the glove compartment. The state trooper came striding up alongside us. After I lowered the power window quickly, he leaned in and asked if I realized how fast I was going, and I said, "Yes, I know I was speeding," as I handed him license and registration.

The trooper went to his car and then came back, handed me the ticket to sign, and as I was signing, asked, "You wouldn't be related to Fred Phelps, would you?"

"Yes, but we are separated."

"Why didn't you tell me before I wrote the ticket?"

"Because I was wrong. I was speeding."

He gave me a curious look. I shrugged. The law was the law, after all. The trooper suggested that I go to court; possibly the points would be decreased or dropped, or perhaps I would only have to pay court fees.

As it turned out, my court date fell on the same day as my interview for the position at Southwest Academy. I decided to take the whole day off and began it by interviewing with Principal Darryl Bonds, a strong, idealistic, yet tough educator on whom I made a positive impression immediately. African American, he was visionary in his approach and his ambitious goals for the direction he wanted to take the predominantly African American student body. He was also looking for can-do team players, particularly an experienced educator with practical curriculum-writing skills for a science magnet program that could be applied countywide. Could I do that?

The answer was "Absolutely." I had written curricula for home economics coursework, though not for a science magnet program. By definition, these "magnet" schools had a focus in certain subjects or curricula and were intended to draw students from beyond the immediate locality. Not only was this exciting to me, there was also no doubt in my mind that this was what I was ready for.

Principal Bonds decided to hire me on the spot. But first he had to clear me through one of his superiors, Dr. Karen Roe, county supervisor for family and consumer sciences, who was housed in the central office area for Baltimore County, on the hill. Rather than wait, he called her while I was sitting in his office and announced, "I have found the person I want to hire for my science magnet, and she knows how to write curricula." He added, "Her name is Debbie Phelps."

Karen Roe, whom I had never met, replied, "You have Debbie Phelps in your office?" Karen knew I'd won Teacher of the Year and was listed among the top ten educators in the country in the subject matter that would impact the curriculum I'd be developing. "Send her up to me and I'll contact human resources and take care of paperwork."

God could not have sent me a better guardian angel and mentor at that time in my life and career than Karen Roe. Somehow I knew that. But before we could meet in person, I had to make my way to traffic court and pay for my speeding ticket.

Fred already knew I'd been given the ticket because Michael had told him during a phone conversation. Fred had asked Michael to put me on the telephone at that time. He wanted to know why I'd let the trooper give me the ticket.

"Why didn't you tell him who you were?"

"Because I was wrong."

Fred offered, "Well, I will go to court with you."

"No," I insisted, "you don't have to go to court with me."

I thought I'd made my feelings clear on this, but when I arrived at the courthouse, lo and behold, who was there but Fred.

Now, I know he was trying to do something kind and actually loving and supportive, but I didn't want special treatment. So I tried to just slide in. No such luck, as he came over and stood along-side the row where I was sitting. The courtroom started to fill up as I waited on the bench to be called to approach the judge and pay my debt. And Fred, in his state trooper uniform, was leaning up against the wall, trying to make conversation with me. I'm thinking, *This can't look right for me to be in trouble and trying to curry favor with an officer of the law.*

Fred finally saw my discomfort and left the courtroom. Or so I supposed. But the next thing that happened, when the court official entered and called numbers off the docket to stand and be dismissed or called forward, told me otherwise. As soon as I heard my number and then my name, I stood for a second before I heard a resounding "Dismissed!"

Fred had "pulled a string" (or two or three) and had my ticket dismissed. I didn't like it. At the least I should have pled my case and cited my excellent driving record. I know he meant well, but I felt like a heel in front of all those people who had seen us talking earlier—especially when, from the front row, I had to turn and walk out of the courtroom. It was humiliating!

Not that I held on to those thoughts. Others presented themselves.

As the years would go by, every time Fred and I saw each other, I would still have a mix of feelings. But the speeding ticket encounter would stand out as one of the most complicated. Fred was trying to be kind, he did love me, and I know that in his own way he was in a lot of pain.

Then again, I didn't want or need special treatment. Besides, I had other priorities to think about—a new, challenging job that appeared to be in the offing and the inimitable Karen Roe to meet. From the moment I entered her office, a window of new possibilities and broader vistas opened wide for me. With summer coming, I had a blank canvas on which to design an innovative curriculum. She gave me a laptop, access to all the resources in her office, as well as resources from Penn State and other colleges and universities, and whatever else I needed to develop the course of study. Then we would pilot it in the fall at Southwest Academy and take it out across the county.

On every level, this job was heaven-sent. The salary was better, I was closer to home, and both Darryl Bonds and Karen Roe trusted me. They were going to let me do my thing. It was a wonderful way of being brought into a county and into the system.

Karen Roe, very proper, very poised, was the right role model at the right time. We were alike in so many, many ways, both believers that all children could learn and both color-blind when it came to student achievement. I admired how she invariably chose her words thoughtfully, always operating at a high level of sophistication. Karen also recognized my aspirations to one day move into a supervisory role and looked for every opportunity to showcase my accomplishments to her colleagues and others.

So once again, the seasons changed, a summer full of possibilities gave way to a very busy fall in 1995 with the rolling out of the program I'd developed and a new team at Southwest Academy that I would guide and mentor. My home team consisting of me, Hilary, Whitney, and Michael was in the process of finding our way, dealing with a handful of issues that were still challenging, learning how to make those all-important life adjustments. There was a lot of pinch-hitting and improvising, joy and love, plus a need for patience and commonsense problem solving. That's a normal family by any standard. True, we all had some seriously lofty goals up ahead of us that we had the audacity to believe we could accomplish.

In those winter months that preceded the Olympic trials in March 1996, another Charles Dickens title comes to mind that tells you exactly where we were headed next and what we were all feeling at the time—*Great Expectations*!

~~~~~

EIGHT

Teachable Moments

Here is an excerpt from an unfinished journal entry I began on Sunday, March 3, 1996, the evening before Whitney's departure for the United States Olympic Team trials held at the Indiana University Natatorium in Indianapolis:

> *This weekend has been a long one. Hilary and Michael left Thursday for Annapolis. The Maryland Junior Olympic All-Star Meet was at the U.S. Naval Academy. The meet started on Friday. Hilary was swimming the 100-yard butterfly to make another Junior National cut and Michael swam the entire weekend to qualify for the 1996 Maryland All-Star Team.*

Hilary's time in the 100 didn't qualify for Juniors. She was told that it would hurt, and she said it did. Michael had a very successful meet. . . . He placed first in everything he swam and broke every meet and state record.

All three of us were anxious to get back to Towson . . . drove through a McDonald's, got gas (nearly on empty), and came home. As we unpacked we shared cards, gifts, and best wishes to Whitney . . . .

Michael is tired, big-time. He felt bad that he didn't have an opportunity to get Whitney a good luck gift this weekend at the meet. So he made Whitney one of his famous cartoon people that had a pair of goggles in his hands. On the back he wrote a nice note to Whitney that expressed his feelings.

As if it was yesterday, I am back in that night trying to gauge where we were in the next leg of our journey, on the eve of those very great expectations, while noting that we seemed to be in a stable place with all endeavors.

We did, however, have a few instances of the kids seeing how far they could push me. For instance, Hilary had crashed a car, had had a fender bender or two, had snuck out of the house once, and had thrown a party when I was away at a swim meet. (She and her friends had cleaned up afterward, but they did such a good job that I became suspicious when I realized there was nothing in the garbage cans.) She had pushed the envelope on a few other occasions too.

Early on as a single parent, I decided to be very collaborative with my children. It's not really in my vocabulary to tell someone a flat-out no anyway. My style is to lead by example and coax the other person to come to the conclusion that makes the most common sense. There may have been a few incidents when I used no and it backfired, so that was the most practical approach for me. One time Hilary wanted to go to a midnight movie on a weekend night. Instead of saying no, I asked, "Well, do you really want to go to this midnight showing when you have practice tomorrow?" She thought about that. I went on, "What if you oversleep or don't swim well?" I told her to think it over and I left the room.

Well, my strategy didn't work, and Hilary left the house and went to the movie. I truly hadn't thought there was a phantom of a chance she would do that. After I sat and thought about it, I realized that she hadn't made a good choice, so I went to the theater, asked the person at the box office if I could enter for just a minute or two, and was allowed to go into the dark theater, where I tapped her on the shoulder and whispered, "You need to come home." And she did.

Maybe she, like her sister and brother, sensed that I was on my own learning curve as a single mom, and they were being as patient with me as I was trying to be with them. In any case, by March 1996, Hilary, the pioneer, was now blazing a new path—to college! In the last months leading up to high school graduation, she was more or less set to go to the University of Richmond, scholarship and all! Since she was going to attend a summer session, it was my hope to get her to senior beach week and home, safe and secure, without any controversies.

At this time Michael and I were also in collaborative mode. He was dealing with so much so consistently and in basically such a good-natured manner—adjusting to the medication that seemed to be helpful, working extra hard in school and in the swimming pool—that he rarely if ever tried my patience. There was an instance during a meet when he was out-touched by a little guy who had come from nowhere to win—in a contest that Michael really should have and could have won. Furious, after touching in second and realizing that he had lost, he threw both his goggles and his cap, pulled himself up onto the pool deck, and stormed off. I couldn't believe my eyes.

Instead of blasting him on the spot, which I'd seen plenty of parents do, I waited until we were ready to drive home and could talk about it calmly. When I was in charge of a carpool and had other children in tow, we used to call this combination of driving and talking "field trips." Our discussions could be fun, instructive, yet also frank. My question was simply, "So how do you think you did today?"

Michael's typical response was usually something to the effect of "Okay." But when I asked about one specific race, he knew exactly which one I was referencing, and he quickly admitted that he didn't like the finish and that he had made an unwise choice in throwing a tantrum. Then, as usual, I told him that I agreed and expected much more sportsmanlike behavior from him as my son, a representative of our family and North Baltimore, oh, and, I had to add, "I don't ever want to see you do that again." And I didn't—except once, under much different circumstances.

Bruce High School yearbook staff

Bruce High School's Archives Court, in which I had the honor of being crowned Archives Queen.

Serving as the state secretary, I traveled to Los Angeles for the Future Homemakers of America national conference while in high school.

A magical moment in my life, when I was given Fred's fraternity pin. His fraternity brothers sang to me as part of the tradition.

A bright-eyed Hilary is ready to take on the world.

Being a mother is the most important thing to me. Here I am with Hilary, trying to stay warm.

Providing life lessons at an early age; Hilary is meeting her grandfather Pap for the first time.

Life is generational: three generations sharing quality time—my mother, me, and the newest member of the Phelps family, Hilary.

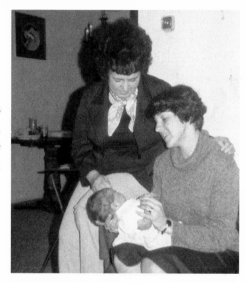

Whitney having fun while climbing on playground equipment in Frederick during our trip to western Maryland to visit our families.

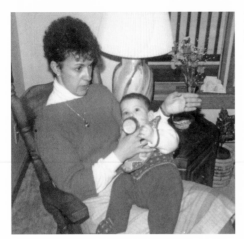

Here I am giving Michael his bottle. He has always had a big appetite!

Fred holds a young Michael at the dining-room table.

Inquisitive Michael as he awakes from an afternoon nap.

The family dressed in our best! Hilary, me, Michael, and Whitney on Easter Sunday, heading to church.

Michael tries to read a book bigger than he is!

Big sister Hilary and little brother Michael playing in the snow in Whiteford, Maryland; fun time together.

Having fun in the sun in Ocean City, Maryland. We were always around water.

Michael's catch of the day! As a kid, Michael asked
questions about everything.

Hilary, Michael, and Whitney pose on photo day at the
North Baltimore Aquatic Club.

Michael and Whitney on Christmas morning. Michael has always been protective of his older sisters.

Whitney, Hilary, and Michael celebrating together with a piece of cake for Hilary's birthday.

Hilary, Michael, and Whitney pose for a photo op at the
North Baltimore Christmas swim meet.

Whitney, Michael, and Hilary on vacation at the beach with
several other swim families.

Whitney returns from Senior Nationals after competition. What a butterflier!

Michael smiles as he and his sisters compete in the family relay at the
Blue & Gold meet. Where's mom?

Having a mother-daughter moment
with Hilary.

Capturing a special moment at a family celebration.

Photograph by Lisa O'Shea

Here is Michael (with coach Bob Bowman) being announced as a member of the 2000 Olympic team.

Here I am in front of the Sydney Opera House.

Baltimore County Public Schools Office of Communications

With superintendent Anthony "Tony" Marchione. I was one of the top five finalists for the Baltimore County public schools Teacher of the Year award.

My students mean the world to me. Here we are on a school trip.

Photograph by Kurt Graser

Whitney, Michael, and Hilary at the Baltimore Ravens game
after the Beijing Olympics.

That early goggles incident was definitely a teachable moment for both of us.

Around this time, I was having plenty of teachable moments at Southwest Academy, where I was implementing the program I'd designed the previous summer. The school was on the line between the Baltimore City proper and Baltimore County school districts and was as close an urban setting as I had worked in up to that time. I was anxious to invest my heart and soul in creating the success Darryl Bonds had in mind in rebuilding and reimagining the possibilities for this school. But it took some adjustment for me to come from the more affluent, mainstream suburbs of Bel Air, with its students named Meredith, Morgan, Thomas, and John, and get to know my new students, who had more unusual names such as Muffai and Taisha.

While the school was predominantly African American, there were also large numbers of children of immigrant and other minority backgrounds. On my first day I was amazed at what looked like the United Nations—a wide mix of ethnicities, unfamiliar accents, terminology, and lingo, all coming together in loud conversations. The volume was on high all the time! And then I arrived in my classroom to find forty-plus students in one class. Luckily some of my other classes had a more manageable number.

But I was learning fast and loving every minute, determined to make it work. I found a leadership role for myself in the collaborative mix as well, both in the classroom and as a voice of experience for many of the younger teachers. Adding to our challenges, representatives from the state offices and neighboring counties came around frequently to inspect our progress or lack thereof. This only made me even more determined to contribute to the success that I knew was achievable.

As for determination, the person most on my mind when I began my journal in March 1996 was Whitney. We had now been at NBAC for almost nine years, and she'd had Olympic dreams in her head from as far back as the first time she hit the water and took off like a rocket. As much as we were told not to overemphasize the O word, envisioning the ultimate mountain peak—she was named after Mount Whitney, after all—had become part of our family identity.

As confident as we were, it had been a rough road that I was only beginning to get past. In time, Whitney would piece together what really had been going on for the last four years, from the time she was twelve.

Unlike her siblings, who tended to be more open with their emotions, at least with loved ones, Whitney was more of an introvert, keeping everything clamped down tight. Or as she later said, "I just didn't think anyone needed to hear my problems." That would change in later years, and I'd be able to get a clearer picture of how her desire to be lighter and thinner—so that she could swim faster— had slowly become an eating disorder. I wondered in the beginning if she was hearing the same remarks I overheard when Hilary first started developing as a teenager and one of the coaches remarked, without really thinking, "Oh, no, she's getting boobs! Well, her career is over."

I knew overtraining and overdieting were an issue among young gymnasts and dancers, to the point that growth and development could be impaired. But until that remark, it hadn't occurred to me that being thin was a priority in the swimming arena. In my view, there were plenty of female champions with hourglass figures or curves who excelled and medaled. I was taken aback by that remark but let it go.

For Whitney, it seemed that a combination of comments had left an impact. The first of these came from a coach when she was twelve or so and eating french fries after a meet when he quipped, "That's the last time you will be eating those!"

To a young athlete with exceptional determination and discipline, a coach's word often becomes gospel. So she started cutting back on certain less nutritious foods—the junk, fried, and sugary stuff. Whitney saw the immediate benefits. She did get stronger, leaner, and faster. At that formative time when self-image is connected to slimness and fitting into mini-sized clothes, she must have also started getting compliments from her peers. Since Whitney was competing and winning on larger stages, she was also having her photo taken, and so staying "camera thin" became an asset too.

No red flags for me at the time. Long before there were excesses, she went on a diet followed by many elite athletes that emphasized protein and cutting out starchy carbohydrates but included healthy fats. Whitney took this diet up those three notches, as she usually did with her swim practice training, and started cutting out everything—all fat, most protein—and eating increasingly smaller portions. The fact that this was also a time of instability, ups and downs at home, probably fueled the focus that she had on not eating. As an adult, Whitney recalled, "Every day I thought about how I could eat less than yesterday. It was the only thing that I could control, and I needed to control something."

Because growing bones need nutrients more than ever in those years, the toll on her body was dire—to the point that she developed osteoporosis in her early teens. By the time we finally understood what she was going through, the initial benefits of weight loss were no longer happening. As a matter of fact, she was becoming weaker, more injury-prone, and, unbeknownst to me, at times unable to practice. In competition, her swim times weren't improving. She wasn't losing races necessarily, but she wasn't bettering her time on the events in which she was, at fifteen, one of the highest-ranked swimmers in the world. Her solution was to soldier on, pushing herself to exhaustion.

I should have known earlier that the complaints Whitney began to articulate about back pain were much more serious than they seemed. Again, it goes to show just how high her pain tolerance was and how powerful her determination was that she didn't make a bigger deal about back and shoulder injuries that would only get worse. Whitney wasn't alone. There were other girls at her swimming level who were dieting excessively and suffering injuries. Plus, the training regimens in that era were extreme. Even when Michael was training at his highest levels, he never did the kind of sets at his age that Whitney was doing at hers.

To compound her obstacles, there had been that incident at one of the two meets in Paris (both times I was unable to go with her) when Whitney had slipped and fallen off a swim block, hurting her back. It was a lesson for me, not that it could have been prevented. But when everything came to light, I regretted that I wasn't there when she went through the ordeal, and I decided that thereafter I was going to find a way to be in the stands, if at all possible, when my children were swimming in big meets.

Nine months or so out from Olympic trials, not long after Whitney's fifteenth birthday, what had been becoming more and more obvious could no longer be ignored. A coach turned to me at a meet while watching Whitney on the blocks and leaned toward me, saying, "She looks *thin*." She shook her head, letting me know this was a cause for concern.

The next comment came from ten-year-old Michael, who mentioned in passing that every time Whitney—a wonderful cook—whipped him up something to eat or packed him a lunch, she wasn't making anything for herself.

It was Murray Stephens who called to inform me of the concern. When I first broached the subject with Whitney, I put it to her without judgment, saying, "Michael doesn't understand why you're not eating."

Whitney shrugged, sort of denying that it was a problem; she wasn't ready to hash it out. We next consulted with a nutritionist who specialized in eating disorders. A healthier eating plan was devised, and every night Whitney and I sat down in my bedroom to review what she had eaten that day, and then we filled out a sheet posted on my bedroom door that listed what she ate, how much, and how she felt after eating. Whitney went along with the program—or so I thought. Later she admitted to the nutritionist and to me that she had not been telling the truth and had exaggerated or made up how much she was actually eating. Whenever she figured out that I had snuck extra butter and cream into her mashed potatoes and resorted to other tactics that the nutritionist had suggested to add calories to her intake, Whitney only nibbled. Then she went to her room and did extra sit-ups and jumping jacks.

As she told me years later, though the eating disorder wasn't the cause of her back problems, she suspected it was the reason for the severity of the damage and the duration of the pain. One reason she would eventually break her silence about how she became anorexic (bordering on bulimic later on) was to send a message to young athletes that there is a healthy way to eat that can improve energy and peak performance without becoming extreme and self-destructive. Her own education in that area was still to come, something she would pursue with the same focus and passion she invested in her swimming.

As in other regards, Michael was paying attention to his sister's lessons and incorporating them at a deep level. When he was given an assignment in school to write an essay about a personal hero, he didn't have to search very far for someone he wanted to claim as "My Hero":

My hero is my sister, Whitney Phelps. I have known her all my life. . . . My sister possesses so many outstanding personality traits that I can't even name them all, but here are some I admire. She is generous because she makes me food when I am hungry. She is also determined because she fell off a swim block in Paris and hurt her back but she is giving all she has to get back into training every day.

Michael was exceedingly proud of both of his sisters, but this time he chose to write about Whitney, he said, because "she stands out," because she was "caring" and "very bright," and because "when things get hard, she always gives it all she has."

So, with all that going for her, now that the much-anticipated Olympic trials were upon us, I wanted to believe that Whitney was in a much better place. To rekindle a love for cooking and for food, as well as to find a way to exert control, she had started an ongoing project of collecting and organizing recipes. Indeed, in my journal entry the night she told me, I noted

Whitney is copying recipes for her recipe file. She shares with me that she would like to work this summer at a bagel place . . . and earn money for car insurance. She did say if she made the Olympic Team she would want to work later.

That was Whitney not getting ahead of herself, amazingly so. That evening I was calm and grateful, reflecting on how much I loved knowing that Michael—champion sleeper—was going to bed happy that Whitney loved his drawing, and how Hilary, now play-ing on the computer, chatting on the phone with a friend, had been so proud when she hugged her sister hard and tears had filled her eyes. And then there was Whitney, as I wrote, "Cool, calm, collected, at ease, and ready to swim," who was closing up her recipe file and adding the last items to her suitcase.

The sounds in the house at 624 West Chesapeake Avenue reminded me of sitting poolside during a morning practice—everyone active but focused, in their own lanes, moving forward in fluid fashion. We were safe, secure, and hopeful.

On the other hand, confession time in my dear diary followed: I was a nervous wreck! With a capital N! After I checked with Whitney—for the umpteenth time—about whether she had remembered to pack this item or that, she said, "Mom, I'm just going to a swim meet." She sounded exactly like Murray Stephens, who reinforced that phrase over and over as D-day approached. I was even more in awe that she could be so cool—especially with all the coverage that Whitney Phelps was getting, including making the cover of an insert in the newspaper!

It was all well and good to take that "let's wait and see" attitude, but then I noted, "Boy, it sure does get a lot of advertisement for a swim meet."

In any case, what really mattered, as I wrote to myself once the girls had gone to bed and Michael was fast asleep, and I prepared to put down my pen and turn out the lights:

I love my kids and I'm so very proud of each of them. They're super and I've been blessed. Good night and sleep tight!

Next morning, March 4, we hit the ground running at 5:30 a.m., with Hilary starting earlier in the kitchen making breakfast, Whitney on the phone with her boyfriend, then the arrival of fellow swimmer Anita Nall (a 1992 gold-medal-winning Olympian) and Anita's dad to pick up Whitney at 6:45 a.m. After loading her suitcase into the car, Whitney—swim bag over her shoulder, a patriotic bunny for good luck in her hands—turned to me, knowing I was fighting the tears. I snapped some photos of her and Anita, along with Mr. Nall, who in his white shirt, dark suit, and black wool coat looked like an actual chauffeur. We laughed about that so that I didn't cry, and then I waved good-bye, standing outside for as long as I could handle the cold before dashing inside to grab my things and head off to work. Hilary, in her last year of high school, would be responsible for getting Michael to school on time.

On the Beltway, backed up in traffic, I worried about which way Mr. Nall had taken to go to the airport, concerned that they might miss their flight. Dashing into Southwest Academy five minutes before the bell—so unlike me—I was amazed by the well-wishing that came from students and staff members. During the first period, there was an announcement made on the public address system from the office to wish Whitney much success in Indianapolis at the Olympic trials. That was only the beginning. As the day went on, the excitement built with handwritten cards and banners turning up in my classroom, in the refrigerator I kept for food science projects, and in the teachers' lounge. Unbelievable. So was the fact that I suddenly thought I was having a heart attack. Just kidding. Even so, wow, the blood was pumping!

Fortunately, a colleague reassured me that it was only anxiety. But it was anxiety with a capital *A*! Calming myself down, I made it home, returned phone calls, handled mail, and made dinner, then picked up Michael from swim practice, before heading back to the house:

> *I wanted to go to sleep and Michael wanted to watch* Angels in the Outfield, *so we camped out in Whitney's room. I was freezing, so Michael covered me up with four or five blankets. I fell asleep, he ate dinner and watched the movie . . . came up to say Whitney was on the voice mail. He thought Hilary was going to get it but she was in the shower. . . . Whitney left a message and said she'd call back on Tuesday. . . .*
>
> *I'm going back to sleep now because I'm stressed!!! But Whitney, you don't know that and I don't plan to let you know until it's all over! I love you all.*

In the days that followed, I directed my words less to myself— except when confessing that I was nervous—and more to Whitney, as though she could feel all our love and support coming through the pages in the journal. On Wednesday, March 7, I was encouraged by news from Cathy Lears about how the trials were going. If I had any concerns, they didn't show up when I jotted down my belief that "Whitney is tough and ready and she will prove it in a few days." Then, cheerfully, I signed off with an old standby—"Nightee Peepers!"

On Thursday, March 8, I have entries describing Michael's nervous excitement and how he wished he could fly into Indianapolis with me and my brother, B.J., rather than waiting to come in later in the weekend with Hilary in time for Whitney's big moment on

Tuesday. Oh, yes, and more of an outpouring of hope and congratulations from everyone at school, including one of my sixth graders who had declared, "Mrs. Phelps, Whitney is the bomb!" (I translated this in my journal to make sure that whoever perchance read it would know it meant "hot!")

On Friday, March 10, I detailed my departure from a snowy Baltimore, the rush to the airport, the wait on the plane while the wings were de-iced, and the fun of sitting in first class—for only the second time in my life—with B.J. A second entry for the day included mentions of the thrill of watching some of the finals and celebrating the successes of other NBAC teammates. After "the great experience of eating at Hooters"—yes, I meant that sincerely after I tasted the delicious chicken wings—I had the chance at last to see Whitney and to remind her how incredible it was that she had made it this far. She vented, needing to shake off some of her nerves, but overall I felt certain that she was prepared and that her concerns were normal. That night, my next-to-last entry was directed to my favorite second-born daughter:

> Well, cutie pie, I'm going to sign off. I hope you swim well tomorrow. I hope your stroke feels good and that you're pleased with your performance.

I began writing early on Saturday, March 9, 1996, by expressing my realization that all Whitney needed to do was to swim the 100-meter butterfly that day and get rid of her jitters. Her real test wouldn't come until Tuesday, March 12, when the 200-meter butterfly was scheduled. I had all my fingers and toes crossed for her, almost literally. Resorting to being the mom on the team, I did remind myself—and later Whitney—that I didn't know what she was aiming for timewise on the 100 fly. In fact, I usually don't have in my head the numbers, times, and records that my children have achieved before or are trying to improve upon. Just before my words trailed off midsentence and this chronicle came to an end, I made this wish:

I want to see a swim that keeps your goggles on your face, a good start, a good finish, and a nice long stroke.

From what I could tell, that's what she swam! Since she wasn't expected to place first or second on this short-distance speed race, coming in seventeenth wasn't bad at all. Moreover, as any first-timer to Olympic trials knows, every race is a learning experience, and this one gave her a feel for the water and the field. The sentiment going into Tuesday for the 200 was that Whitney could hold her own, as she had a year earlier in the same pool for the World Championships when she did just okay in the morning preliminaries but came back in the evening to swim the finals and took three seconds off her time to win.

From every indication, we were about to see a repeat of the same story on March 12, 1996. In the morning prelim, Whitney swam the same time as the year before. Hilary and Michael, now in the stands with us, expressed their confidence that she was holding back for the finals. As hopeful as we were, the hours that ticked by until the evening arrived moved much too slowly for my liking. At last the moment was upon us. I remember glancing around and looking at the faces of every nervous, hopeful family member or coach—much as I had at every meet and every race since Hilary had first led us down the primrose path to the swimming pool—and for the first time I realized the magnitude of being at this level. This was a pinnacle to be celebrated, no matter what, I reminded myself. That was true for every swimmer in every lane and in the entire venue.

For us, it had been nine years to reach this opportunity that would be over in about two minutes. And then we would build upon it, regardless. Even before the race was over, during which I lived and died a few lifetimes, I finally knew the true meaning of a phrase that's worth filing away for all of us for many future uses:

> The thrill of victory and the agony of defeat: you won't truly know one without the other.

From the outset, when Whitney dove into the pool, she looked to be in top form, on her game. At the last turn, the 150-meter mark, she was still holding even with the field—as she always swam this race. Her forte was to then exert the pressure and speed up in that last fifty meters, just as she had a year earlier. When she came into the wall, at first I didn't know whether she had pulled ahead or not. Everything happened so quickly and everyone was reacting differently. One of her coaches whisked by me en route to the pool deck, shaking his head as he said, "She's two seconds off. That's not going to cut it."

Then I looked back down at the pool at Whitney. She had come in sixth at a time of 2:14:13. The second-place time was 2:12:45. A difference of 1.68 seconds prevented her from making the Olympic

Team that would compete in Atlanta, Georgia, in the coming summer. Whitney was the last to get out of the pool.

Some months later, when she arrived at the University of Richmond, Hilary wrote about what she recalled of that day and the weeks that followed:

> *I had never seen my little sister and my best friend so devastated in all of her life. She tried hard not to cry but she couldn't help it and neither could we. I tried to joke around with her but this was one time when she didn't want to hear it. She tried to smile and laugh but she couldn't. . . .*
>
> *Now I'm more determined. I use her as my motivation. It's sort of my way to help her. She didn't do it, so I want to do it for her. It's not the Olympics, but maybe she'll be as proud of me as I am of her.*

As for myself, there was no way to be philosophical or fatalistic about the many lessons learned from this experience. We all hurt so much for Whitney. It was like a death in the family. Regardless of the warning signs, everyone had assumed that she was a shoo-in.

From that day forward, I could not say anything to Whitney about not making the team. It was another ten years before she brought it up by thanking me for giving her the space to work through everything her way. She told me that if there was one thing that I had taught her it was that time—such a powerful force in our lives in so many ways—heals most wounds.

What Whitney did bring up to me as soon as we returned to Baltimore was "I have to go to the doctor."

"Why?"

"My back is killing me."

We went to several orthopedists who diagnosed her as having a herniated disk and multiple stress fractures. That was the first I knew about how much she had been masking her pain. But when a short while later Whitney reported that she wanted and needed to get back in the water, resolved to return full-time to training, I figured it must not be as dire as we had been told and I supported that decision. She was about to take her signature level of determination and crank it up many notches higher.

Before Olympic trials, every top swimming college had been making overtures to recruit Whitney. An A/B student, she had been the only Phelps to become involved with a marvelous creative program called Odyssey of the Minds that put together teams of students who approached a variety of subject matter in detective fashion—sending them into museums, libraries, and laboratories all across Baltimore for research. She had loved it. I was excited about where higher education would take her and knew that, as an Olympian, she would find doors opened for her at any college of her choice with a full scholarship and ride.

After word got out about the seriousness of Whitney's injuries, even though she was training again, letting her coaches and everyone else know that she would be back in action for 2000, the college offers evaporated.

I didn't know what to do. But Whitney did. And I was going to have to trust that.

I was also going to have to listen more to the words of Santa Claus, who left a lengthy note for Hilary, Whitney, and Michael

Phelps that following Christmas, encouraging them to "Remind your mom that she works too hard. She needs to relax a little."

Santa was very articulate that year:

Hilary, keep up the great work academically and athletically. That UR record you broke in 1000 freestyle was really great! . . . Whitney, I see you have been working this year and just cooking up a storm. I heard you had a sore back. You had better take care of yourself. . . . Oh, by the way, I was looking for a kangaroo to put under the tree but I left them in Australia. Maybe you can get one over there when you go to Sydney. . . . Michael, what a great interim you brought home this last time. . . . And that Christmas meet you swam in was pretty cool. You just swim too fast but that's okay. . . . Well, I have to leave. Take care and keep a smile on those beautiful (Whitney and Hilary) and handsome (Michael) faces. XO Santa. P.S. Include your mom in that beautiful face stuff too.

I may not yet have been as undeniably cheerful as my alter ego, Santa Claus, but I was pulling up again from the depths of despair that we'd all felt that day in Indianapolis. We were all seasoned and wiser from the letdown, perhaps having learned the lesson that Whitney coined—that some things don't happen for a reason.

If anyone had predicted that we would be back in Indianapolis, same place, same pool, four years later for Olympic trials again and celebrating a Phelps thrill of victory in making the U.S. Olympic team, I might not have believed it. Then again, why not?

NINE

~~~~~

History 101

The ironic part of great expectations is that every now and then, even after those moments when you feel that they've slipped from your grasp, they have a funny way of coming true in a place and time when you were least expecting them. That's what happened with the 2000 Olympic Games in Sydney, Australia. I had to pinch myself to make sure I wasn't dreaming when our flight landed there on the other side of the globe! The experience was a gift, for many reasons. The real irony was that when Bob Bowman first arrived in North Baltimore and shortly thereafter made a series of wild predictions that eventually came true, Sydney was not even part of the game plan—or what he would call in large-scale goal-setting terms "the platform."

There is a saying that when the student is ready, the teacher appears. No doubt Bob Bowman was the teacher who appeared just when Michael was ready—on May 5, 1997, to be precise, a little more than a month before Michael's twelfth birthday. You could also tweak the saying to "When a swim family is ready, the coach appears." That was true in our case. It didn't take long for me to hit it off famously with Bowman, who understood how important family would always be on Team Phelps.

In later years, when sports analysts and others marveled over Michael's natural abilities and some even suggested that anybody could have coached him and achieved the same spectacular results, Bowman would say, "Well, it may be true that anybody could coach Michael, but not anybody could coach Debbie Phelps!"

Of course he was joking, but the truth is that he was as much a cheerleader for me as I was for everyone else. He was sensitive to my role as a single parent at the same time that he made sure to confer with Fred and with me over any major strategies he had up his sleeve. Bob respected the family history with swimming and understood the value of the things Michael had learned from observing both Hilary and Whitney. He also recognized that we'd been going through a rough ride and that it was time to write a new chapter.

As it so happened, Bob had come to North Baltimore to do the same thing. Originally from South Carolina, he used his southern wit and charm to mask the intensity he brought to several passions—including music, raising Thoroughbred racehorses, and coaching young swimmers. Add to that mix the kindest heart, a perfectionist streak that rivaled mine, and the most scathing dose of sarcasm, and you have a sense of the complicated, multilayered young coach who was the first to look me square in the eye and ask if I had any idea how much potential my son had and how far he could go.

In time, it would be interesting to learn that Bob's hero was not a swimmer or an athlete. His hero had always been Leonard Bernstein. "I thought he was a genius," Bob once told me, confiding, "I wanted to conduct the New York Philharmonic." Then he joked, "That was my goal until your child ruined it for me."

But the conducting metaphor lasted; those who knew Bob and his approach thought of him as much like a genius conductor and Michael as the virtuoso musician. After someone later called Michael Phelps the Mozart of swimming, who makes everything look effortless even though it's not, Bob said, "If he's Mozart, then I'm Beethoven. For me, everything is a struggle to get it right, a painful process, as it is for the rest of us."

For all his talk of struggle, there was one thing Bowman had in pure, power-packed concentrate, and that was his belief. His greatest task with Michael was teaching him to have that too. Later on during a challenging interlude in training, he explained why the task was so difficult by using the example of a scene in the movie *Star Wars: The Empire Strikes Back*. He reminded me of the story in which Luke Skywalker goes to study with the great Jedi master, Yoda, who is training him to mentally lift the spaceship out of the mud. Luke tries and fails, tries and fails—Bob recalled—and then he finally looks up and says, "Nobody can do that!" And Yoda basically tells him, "That is why you failed. Because you don't *believe* it's possible."

Eventually, that's what Bob Bowman did with Michael: he made him believe that no matter what he set out to accomplish, it was possible.

What I most appreciated about his approach was that he coached the total swimmer—the total human being. That was evident from the start. Interestingly, right before coming to North Baltimore, Bob was thinking about giving up coaching. At first, after graduating from Florida State University, where he had done well as a collegiate swimmer, he loved being a coach and recognized it as a natural fit for his high standards and motivational skills. But he became frustrated when he discovered that not everyone shared those high standards. He went through a few jobs, apparently, including one place that fired him and rehired him twice. After the third time when they tried to rehire him, Bob said, "I don't think so."

It was around then that Murray Stephens decided to recruit Bob to come on board at NBAC. Murray had expanded the swim complex at Meadowbrook to include a six-lane indoor long-course pool where year-round training could take place—as even more top swimmers were drawn to train there. Bob was exactly the person Murray wanted to help the next generation of champions to reach their goals. The only problem was that Bowman had decided to quit coaching and had a deal lined up to work as a graduate assistant while he earned his degree in farm management. In return for helping the college with their swim team, he would be earning the princely sum of ten thousand dollars. Murray didn't offer him a ton of money, but it was a few times what the college was offering, so Bob said, "I'm there."

After he started coaching Michael, Bob received an offer of a much higher salary for a swim team in Atlanta. Murray then countered by finally giving him a raise and saying, "That's it. You are coaching Michael for the rest of your life." Not too much later, Bob's renown as a swim coach would begin to turn as many heads as the records Michael started to break.

Before we even got to that stage, I should add, Bob initially took his time in assessing and studying just what made twelve-year-old Michael tick. The first time he asked to speak to Fred and me together, it was to say that our son undoubtedly had talent and immense potential. And without saying it, he let us know that Michael was starting to cause a stir in the swimming world. He was on the radar, so to speak, especially as he began to win against older swimmers. But Bob was careful to let us know there were lots of twelve-year-olds who exploded onto the scene in early adolescence and then never amounted to anything. The key would be consistency, normalcy, and a love for the sport. He wanted us to slowly wean Michael off other sports—lacrosse, baseball, soccer—not all at once, but in due time.

I understood what Bowman was saying, but I believed that if Michael really was passionate about swimming, he would give up the other sports on his own.

The next time I spoke to Bob, the tone was very similar, only this time he said, "We need to start planning." Again, we were going to keep things normal, structured, and focused. But based on the calculations he'd carefully written down on a piece of paper, assuming that Michael kept working and improving as he had been, we could expect he would hit his swimming stride by 2004, build on it by

2008, and then make history by 2012. Since Chicago was bidding to be the Olympic host in 2012, the plan assumed that Michael would be performing his best in the United States. The sky was the limit. Actually, there was no limit.

That was crazy talk. We had lived through the disappointment of thinking that Whitney was a shoo-in for the Olympics, so I couldn't go there. But Bob was the coach, obviously, and we would be supportive. The teacher in me had to add, "As long as it doesn't interfere with his grades. I want him to be successful in middle school and we've been working on that. I'm a firm believer that athletics and academics go hand in hand."

Bob agreed. We'd take it one step at a time, building the skills, planting the seeds, laying the foundation for his plan. He was talking my language! The only thing he warned of was that if we weren't careful, if we either pushed too hard or didn't give Michael the challenges he needed, as well as the opportunity to be a kid, it could all go the other way.

From that point on, I believed. Not only that, I relaxed—perhaps in a way that I had never been able to do with the girls. Bob reminded me of myself in a few respects, both in having that type A personality and in reaching out to parents to become partners in their children's success. He was doing with me what I did with the parents of my middle school students. Without saying it in so many words, he helped to reinforce my strengths: being the mom on the team, always there, no matter what; working hard and doggedly refusing to give up; and never losing sight of the joy for life and sport that matters most. He also noticed that whenever I watched Whitney swim, I was knotted up and tense, as if I were in the pool swimming for her, and that emotional investment wasn't healthy for me or for Whitney. With Michael, Bob soon taught me that I had no control over his performance and that if he didn't win a particular race or better his time, there was always the next race. This was an important lesson I hadn't learned earlier.

His words of wisdom coincided with a period of personal growth for me. I could feel a weight lifted off me, and that feeling carried over to other areas, where it was much needed as the daily pace of life started to speed up. After a while, whenever stress did occur, I thought, *Oh well, this is to be expected with me starting another challenging but exciting teaching job, two daughters in college, and a teenage son who was swimming every single day of the year, rain, shine, sleet, snow, flood, or blizzard.* Little did I know that the pace of life was practically a snail's crawl compared to what was still to come!

When Whitney had first returned from Indianapolis and we realized the extent of her injuries—and the fact that all the colleges who might have tried to recruit her were no longer interested—she earned an even greater admiration from me for her definitive brand of determination. Instead of feeling sorry for herself, Whitney went online, on her own, and researched options that had yet to be revealed. Lo and behold, before she was set to graduate from Towson High School, the coach from the University of Nevada, Las Vegas came across country to meet her, signing her for a five-year full ride, injured. She was off and running! I mean that literally, as she added running to her training regimen in the hopes of building back some of her strength without stressing her body too much in the pool.

So before I knew it, I had two daughters in college—my "running rebel" at UNLV and my southern belle at University of Richmond. I was soon being given all sorts of lessons about having faith in God to take care of my girls and about believing in Whitney and Hilary, trusting that they would navigate their journeys successfully. There were a few hiccups along the way. I would never forget the crash course in having a coed that I was given when Hilary went off to the U. of R. and I just prayed that she'd make it through this new phase of independence without any piercings, tattoos, or mishaps. Just when I was almost ready to exhale, I received a phone call from Hilary telling me, "Oh, Mom, I got a tattoo." So did her roommate, a basketball player.

When I asked what kind of tattoo Hilary had chosen, she let me know it was a small shamrock—her birthday symbol, after all.

Her roommate had opted for a tattoo of a jackrabbit.

"Where did the two of you put your tattoos?" I asked.

"Where you will never see them," she assured me.

With Hilary as the trailblazer, as usual, I was prepared when Whitney came home and unveiled her own tattoo, followed later by a pierced tongue and, another time, a tiny diamond in her nose.

Life lessons!

Hilary continued to push forward onto new avenues, navigating different arenas, juggling social life, falling down and pulling herself up again—always resilient, never out for the count, allowing her emotions to be part of who she was. She had disappointments—

like the time, senior year of college, when she wasn't made cocaptain of her swim team. She was among four contenders, none of whom was more qualified than the others, but only three were chosen. But a short time after that, Hilary was thrilled when Michael came to her last meet and helped to count laps. Whitney was competing that same weekend at conference championships. Hilary was disappointed not to have her sister there for her last meet, but that didn't stand in the way of my two girls connecting in years to come and being as close as ever.

While we didn't know it quite yet, Hilary's interests were starting to veer off in a new direction with big, sweeping goals to do more for others—to make the world a better place. Back in high school, her priorities had been more about dressing a certain way, carrying a stylish designer handbag, and other more material, everyday concerns. Not that we don't all aspire to be secure financially and have the freedom of options as to how we dress or live. But her education changed her worldview, and she wanted to make a contribution. It didn't surprise me when she combined her areas of study—sociology and criminal justice—and decided to pursue a profession in the nonprofit sector. Nor did it surprise me when this path of hers also inspired Whitney and Michael in their areas of focus.

Whitney was also experiencing a time of growth and learning. Although her injuries weren't yet resolved, early in her college years Whitney finally reached out to a friend to ask for help with the eating disorder that had never been fully addressed. He directed her to a support group, where she was helped to understand how the issue had developed in the first place and then was given the information and tools for attaining a healthy relationship with food. I could not have been more proud, yet again, of how she approached the challenge head-on, her way. Injuries notwithstanding, her competitive strength returned to a degree, and by early 2000 she began to show signs of being ready to make her trial cut to compete at the Olympic trials in Indianapolis, with hopes of making the team that would be traveling to Sydney.

Because of the way Whitney worked through her difficulties, after we'd all ramped up expectations so high, we all were strengthened and weathered with the knowledge that you just have to take the steps one by one.

Along with my children, my dreams and goals were also expanding—thanks to the freedom given to me at Southwest Academy to build my vision from the ground up. In the five years between 1995 and 2000, as a science magnet teacher and the only experienced teacher on the team, I had the honor of partnering with mentors and mentees as our department became the model for the county. Our interdisciplinary curriculum won statewide and national awards. As always, I loved being in the classroom and being hands-on with students who were discovering skills they didn't know they had and were beginning to see what was possible to attain. Just as much, I loved making sure they had the best resources possible—whether that meant taking on the status quo so that our food science lab was state-of-the-art or educating parents and members of the community to support our work.

In the midst of the personal and professional growth, I don't think I would have known how far I'd come if there hadn't been a

moment there when Fred made overtures for us to get back together. He first floated the idea during a stretch when he had been
suggesting various outings that were always coupled with the sentence "This will be good for the kids." I welcomed the family activities that gave him time to strengthen his relationship with the
children, but as for the two of us reuniting, I wasn't interested. Too
much old history. I had really moved on. Once I came to that realization, my next conclusion was that it was time, now that both
girls were out of the house, to move to a smaller place that would
accommodate me and Michael full-time with enough room for
Hilary and Whitney when they came home during summers and
vacations.

As always, the move revved up my decorating juices—especially
when I found a beautiful three-story townhouse in nearby Rodgers
Forge. Now that Bob Bowman was coaching Michael and life was
in normal, simple mode—as he recommended—I decided to institute a practice that I've since never stopped. I call it having a "Debbie day.'" Once a month on a Saturday, depending on activities at
work or with family, I would carve out some "me time." It might
only be two hours or it could be the whole day. It could sometimes
be related to work or family but the objective of Debbie day was to
be as creative, fun, and relaxed as possible. On that day, no matter
what, I always take my watch off so I can't monitor the time. Over
the years, many friends, family members, and colleagues have insti-
tuted their own Debbie days. Some of them use their own names in
referring to time set aside for themselves, but some have adopted
my terms wholesale, just as they use my initials in talking about
their own DP moments. Here are some things I do on Debbie days.

Feel free to borrow from the following or adapt to your purposes (guys as well as gals):

Manicure and pedicure once a week if possible (do it yourself when on a budget). Hair—highlights and cut or style as needed. (If you're like me, your relationship with your hairdresser is like a marriage; honor it accordingly.) Time spent on the weekend at my desk at school is as good as the spa, allowing me to catch up, enjoy the quiet, and come up with innovative ideas. On one Debbie day in preparation for Christmas, I decided to forgo balls that year and hung cards all over the tree. On my special days I also love browsing in the bookstore, library, or magazine rack for decorating and fashion ideas too. And finally, my favorite thing to do on Debbie day (or more frequently as time allows) is to stop by Chico's and peruse the latest arrivals—which always complement the colors and outfits that I already own. And that was years before I actually became a Chico's model!

Bob Bowman was all for Debbie days. He also understood the need to incorporate fun and find ways for Michael and the other children to take breaks after long, rigorous training hours. Using psychology and motivation, he had a policy that after they finished their sets, they could go play a game or jump in the hot tub. That worked for Michael except at those times when his sets, in his opinion, were much harder than everyone else's.

But Bowman wasn't into negotiating. The deal was firm: before Michael could go chill out with everyone else, he had to finish practice. Sometimes Michael refused and Bob would say that was his choice and he would have to go home. Whenever I heard from my son that he needed to be picked up early, I would make him wait until practice was supposed to be over anyway. Michael was never happy about that, but once he was fourteen years old or so, those occasions started to be fewer and farther between. Until one Saturday morning practice when Bob and Michael locked horns like nothing I'd ever seen.

Apparently it started after Bob had him swimming 5000 meters for time, and Michael stopped because everyone else was getting to do something he wanted to do. Refusing to back down, Michael was worked up and ready to melt down, but Bob reminded him that those were the rules and then, not getting the desired response, kicked him out of practice. The next day when Michael showed up on Sunday morning—always their easy practice—after their warm-up Bob brought out the clock to set it up at the side of the pool. Knowing that the clock was used only for the long swims, Michael realized he had to start the 5000 meter again. Before long everyone else was off to play his favorite game, and he was swimming with all that anger and resentment, as Bob stood his ground. Michael wasn't going to be rewarded for not doing what he didn't do the day before. He needed to make up what he had missed.

Michael not only did a terrible job—according to his coach—but came home so upset that he went into his bedroom and in frustration started to dismantle his desk. I wanted to stay out of this, but I still needed to get to the bottom of what was really going on, so I called Bob, who decided we should have a talk and offered to come right over.

As the mom on the team, I felt for Michael, but I had to let the coach do the coaching. The conversation wasn't very pleasant, with a wound-up fourteen-year-old venting about unfairness, and a type A coach raising his voice to a volume more suited to a large aquatic arena than a dining room table. Finally Bob said, "Let's get out of here."

Not hesitating, Michael followed him out. As I sat there in silence after they left, it occurred to me that I didn't have to fix this problem: the two of them were off to do that together. And I knew that was really what Michael needed more than anything right then, to have someone who believed in him and whom he could trust to be there—even when he wasn't on his best behavior.

Sure enough, they came back several hours later, having spent the whole day together, which didn't happen very often at all. Clearly Bob realized that he needed to give Michael his own version of a Debbie day. He drove out to the country where he kept his race-horses, and the two went walking up to the stalls, talking about non-swim-related subjects, and exploring a world that was different from what Michael was seeing day in and day out. As I heard the report, it seemed that Michael was tentative about coming up to pet the horses and instead befriended a barnyard cat. In Bob's view, Michael was not so different from the young Thoroughbreds who were only beginning their training—more powerful than even they knew, a little wild, full of energy, but really wanting to be loved more than anything else. The cat was more like Bob himself and me for that matter—warm, friendly, wanting to give love. Then again, Bob had some of the racehorse personality too.

Michael came back from his day in the country a changed young man. Perhaps he understood that Bob wasn't being tough and demanding because he was unreasonable or because he was on his own ego trip. The effort was really for Michael. Probably Bob learned a lesson that day too—that even though Michael was starting to see his own possibilities, every now and then he just needed to be a regular teenage boy.

Everything went according to Coach Bowman's platform. From being an amazing eleven- and twelve-year-old, Michael kept on overwhelming the competition, continually bettering his time and his finesse as a thirteen- and fourteen-year-old. He was right on target. But in Federal Way, Washington, where Senior Nationals were held in March 2000, when Michael was three months shy of his fifteenth birthday, Bowman started to wonder if he needed to recalculate his predictions.

In the morning prelims for the 200-meter butterfly, he and Murray watched Michael dive in and swim the first 50 meters faster than they'd ever seen him. Bob said they both turned to each other with the same expression of *Whoa, did you see what I just saw?* Coming in at 1:59:06, Michael ended up breaking the record for fifteen- and sixteen-year-olds that had stood for twenty years, shaving five seconds off the time. All Bob said to Michael was "That's pretty good! Maybe you can swim faster tonight?"

Excited, Michael vowed that he would.

Bob later told me these details, admitting that he had to take a walk to his car and it struck him, *Wow, Michael could make the Olympic team this year.* He had never thought that before; it meant we were four years ahead of time. It was no fluke. That night Michael came back for finals and swam the race even faster at 1:59:00.

When Michael called with the news, I could hear in his voice that this was one of the most exciting events in his swimming career. I had no idea that Bob was as dazzled as we were or that he was starting to think about the possibility of Michael's going to Olympic trials the following August. All I knew was that the two of them were off to the Space Needle and having fun in downtown Seattle.

In anticipation of their return, I decided that a celebration was in order, so even though it was still wintry outside, it gave me joy to break out July Fourth decorations. I lined the walkway to our home and decorated our windows with stars and American flags, then hung up a banner welcoming Michael home with big sparkles and congratulations. Around the same time that they were expected back, I had to run out on an errand, only to discover upon my return that Bob had taken down every last decoration.

"Oh, for goodness' sake," I said to Bowman, pointing out that I wasn't making any more of a fuss than I would for my daughters or my students.

He was not moved. He reminded me that we needed to stick with the plan, even though it was going to start moving much faster now. Bob asked, "What are you going to do next time he wins a race, buy him a car?" Before I could answer, he reiterated, "No stars, no stripes, no O word."

Even though I was not happy that night, it was another vital lesson that allowed me to relax, and that's where I had my head when I traveled to Indianapolis for the Olympic trials in August 2000.

This trip was a far cry from what it had been four years earlier. Then I had been nervous with a capital *N*; now I was grateful with a capital *G*.

I was immensely thankful that Whitney had battled back to make it to the Olympic trials—a feat of pure will and pure determination. I was also thankful that Michael was there to compete for a place on the U.S. Olympic team as well. My one regret was that before she'd made the trials, I had missed seeing Whitney in her last competitive race at conference championships because I'd been at Hilary's last collegiate meet.

It was Whitney who searched her soul and made the decision to withdraw from her events and thereby forgo her chance at going to the Olympics. Later she explained that she felt great pride in having reached goals that others hadn't—for her world rankings, her national and international experiences, the people she had met, and the journey she had traveled. She knew what it was to set goals and to see her hard work, along with determination and sacrifice, pay off. Whitney acknowledged that her back had never healed fully; she'd been informed during a doctor's visit that the disks in her neck were bulging. Putting her focus on healing was what she needed to do next, not injuring herself further.

Since Whitney was still technically a competitor, she had the opportunity to remain on the pool deck and watch the entire competition through to the end, including the men's trials. When Michael qualified to come back that evening for the finals of the 200-meter butterfly, it must have made Whitney especially proud that her little brother was competing in the same event that had taken her so far.

I know that when I watched from the stands, it struck me that the torch was being passed. Then again, as per Bob Bowman's instructions, we had no idea what to expect, so when Michael reminded everyone that he was just going there to swim his best, better his time, and to have fun, there were no worries.

Bowman and Michael never told us what they really expected.

Hilary and I arrived that night to find that our seats were in the stands near the diving well, so we went to stand closer, about midpool, where the security representative immediately told us we couldn't be.

"Two minutes," we said in unison.

He didn't look happy, and when two minutes had passed, he returned to usher us away. "Two minutes," we promised again as the race took off.

There was a very strong field, and when I looked over to see that Michael was fifth at the wall, at 150 meters, with only 50 meters to go, the nerves kicked in for me. "I can't watch!" I told Hilary, and kept my eyes on the scoreboard instead, while she clutched my arm and pointed at Michael, who had suddenly shifted into a higher gear for a closing speed nobody expected.

And lo and behold, in what was declared a "surprise upset," Michael streaked to a second-place win, just behind Tom Malchow. Michael had not only qualified for the 2000 Olympics but he became the youngest member of the U.S. Olympic Team since 1932. When the results were announced and it dawned on Michael that he had done it and he was on his way to Sydney, he stood there for a few beats letting it sink in.

Before anyone else could congratulate him, the first person to make her way over and give him the biggest hug you ever saw was

Whitney. After I turned to hug Hilary, there was little I could say or do but to let my tears of gratitude fall.

Even before Sydney, the whirlwind began. No matter how much you want to downplay expectations, the minute the media starts to make predictions, watch out. Even when you go into a competition with the attitude that it's all going to be a learning experience, regardless of the outcome, nobody can tell you to stand there with all eyes upon you and just relax. Bob knew that, obviously, but he wasn't sure what the best approach would be to counter the nerves. Should he tell Michael to swim the race that he was trained to swim, as they had practiced and timed it all along? The regular strategy was to keep some of his power in reserve and then go all out for the last 50 meters. The elements involved were precision, control, focus. Or, Bob wondered, maybe he should tell him to jump in and "swim like hell."

After the race, Bob asked me what I thought he should have told him. I didn't really know but agreed with Bowman's decision at the time to tell Michael to swim it the way he had been trained to do. After all, Bob's approach was to practice the same way you compete; when it was time to perform, you knew what you were doing and weren't nervous. Obviously one could expect a level of fear to accompany being a first-time Olympian. Not only that, but this was his very first international competition—which is very rare for Olympic swimmers, who usually come up in the international ranks. Though Michael was not overly nervous for his event in Sydney, he did let out a couple of clues that made me think he was feeling some prerace jitters. The first indication was that Michael came out and tied his suit when he got to the blocks. For most of the years that he had been swimming, that was something he'd learned to do long before he walked onto the pool deck. Also unusual was the gesture he made of going over to his U.S. teammate Tom Malchow to wish him well before the race. It may have been a genuinely thoughtful good luck gesture, but I knew at once that it was not what either swimmer needed at a time when they should have been concentrating and getting into their own space, focusing on the competition in their lane.

Sydney would not be the last time Michael wasn't totally prepared at the start of a race. A year later, at the U.S. Open in New York, where I had come as a chaperone for NBAC, one of the swimmers came up to where I was seated and said, "Ms. Debbie, I think Michael forgot his cap and goggles." I insisted that everything was fine and I was sure he had everything he needed. Then I watched as he approached the blocks to stretch, then reach into the pocket of his parka to retrieve his items, and sure enough, he didn't have his cap or his goggles. As he looked up into the stands, he motioned to me that he had forgotten his goggles. All I could do was shrug, letting him know there was nothing I could do.

He went ahead with the race. Fortunately it was the backstroke. A representative from Speedo, a major sponsor at that time, joked that if Michael kept swimming so well without goggles, they were going to see a decrease in goggle sales.

When we got to Sydney, and I was watching Michael prepare to swim the 200-meter butterfly, I had the same feeling that there was nothing I needed to do or could do. This was his time to learn everything he could about competing at this level. As soon as the race went off, he settled into a groove and accelerated to a fifth-place finish. Everyone was excited! For his first time in the international arena, that was huge. Bob later told me he had the feeling that Michael could have won a bronze medal if he had given him the advice to just turn on the jets and go.

But rather than second-guess his decision, Bob wanted to look forward, and shortly after our return, the three of us sat down again at the dining room table to take stock of everything that had happened in Sydney. The first thing Michael talked about was the way the Australians revered their swimming heroes, like Ian Thorpe and Grant Hackett, and how much they appreciated the sport of swimming as a national pastime. He was completely struck by that and couldn't understand why in the United States swimming was only of interest every four years. Bob and I were impressed that Michael felt so passionately about it and found ourselves agreeing with him wholeheartedly.

As we reminisced about what a learning experience Sydney was, one subject in particular didn't come up: how the trip had ended for Michael. Since it was the fall and I had to return to work, I had signed Michael over to Bob's care. At fifteen, the last place he needed to be was in the Olympic village, where the partying and festivities were getting wilder and wilder. My assumption was that they were going to watch the rest of the games, get in some sightseeing, and celebrate a victory well earned. But when Bob went to find Michael, he found him crestfallen by news Fred had sprung on him without warning.

When Michael and some teammates went to the Rocks in Sydney Harbor to visit the AT&T hospitality suite there, Fred stopped by to congratulate him, then introduced Michael to Jackie, announcing that they had recently gotten married.

As for myself, I was somewhat shocked when word traveled back to me in Baltimore that Fred was married again, but it was not the end of my world. However, I felt so bad for Michael that his wonderful celebration was overshadowed. For the rest of the trip, he was notably subdued, as I learned from Bob as well as my brother, B.J., and his wife, Krista, and my sister Amy, all of whom had stayed on in Sydney after me.

When Michael and I talked about the news upon his return to Baltimore, I encouraged him to continue to have a relationship with his father, and in the meantime not to let anything detract from the feeling of accomplishment that he ought to have. I told him, "This is your time, Michael."

And truly, we weren't going to let anything mar the gift that the experience had been. It was the foundation laid for whatever was coming up next. In wanting to make sure that we built on it, Bob Bowman suggested that the three of us sit down for another talk at our dining table in Rodgers Forge. This time he turned to Michael and asked, "So, what do you want to do next?"

Rather than saying he wanted to get in gear for the 2004 Olympic Games in Athens or that he wanted to start training for one event or the other, Michael's simple answer was "I want to break a world record."

The first opportunity for him to do that came along five months later in Austin, Texas, again with the 200-meter butterfly. When Michael asked Bob for his prerace advice, Bowman answered, "Take it out, Michael. Swim as fast as you can."

With a winning time of 1:54:92, Michael not only set a new world's record but in so doing became the youngest world record holder in the history of swimming. Bob now knew what to say whenever it was go time: "Go!"

Four months later, in Fukuoka, Japan, at the 2001 World Championships, using the same strategy to take everything that had been mastered in practice and then going full out, Michael swam the 200-meter butterfly again, this time breaking his own record with a time of 1:54:58.

Not too long after that, Bob started asking Michael on a regular basis what he thought the strategy should be and what he wanted to focus on. That was called coaching the full swimmer. Michael said, "Athens. I want to make the Olympic team, travel to Athens, and win one gold, just one gold medal."

Before that day arrived, Bob decided that in light of how fast everything was moving now, it would be beneficial to expand the team to include the best sports agent that could be found. When he brought Peter Carlisle of Octagon to our attention, Bob was sure he was exactly who we needed. Peter's specialty was extreme sports and Olympic athletes, but more important, he had a wonderful, upbeat energetic manner with just the right temperament for setting certain fires as well as putting out others. He was also a person of character and conviction who recognized how important Michael's family was to Team Phelps. Those were all observations I made later. But Michael was the one who had to decide if he was the right person.

A meeting was set up that I didn't attend. I had missed the meeting with the other agent under consideration, and Bob thought I shouldn't be at this meeting either, because I would be biased toward Octagon. Bob's attitude, as usual, was that if you weren't going to do it one hundred percent, you shouldn't do it at all.

That said, I still wanted the full report. And Bob confirmed that Peter had been very impressive. According to his recap, they held a catered lunch in an elaborate conference room of a law firm. Michael heaped his plate full of food and then dropped it on the floor, much to his embarrassment. Apparently, Peter didn't miss a beat in helping pick it up, making everyone feel very comfortable. Peter then told Michael what they were going to do and how they saw his endorsement opportunities growing and this, that, and the other. As Bob described it, Michael just ate and appeared to be only halfway listening. Finally at the end Peter Carlisle turned to Michael and asked him, "What is it *you* want me to do for you?"

Bob expected Michael to say something a teenager would typically want—perks related to money, status, or privilege, that kind of thing. Instead, Michael looked squarely at Peter and said, "I want you to help me change the sport of swimming."

TEN

~~~

Only Fine on Mondays

The best teachers in the world are those who never stop learning. The person who taught me that was my mother, Leoma Davisson, who in her own way never stopped teaching and never stopped learning. Even in the last seasons of her life, with plenty of health challenges, she greeted every morning as a gift simply because she was able to open her eyes that day, could learn something new, and might possibly pass that learning on to someone else.

Gran loved each and every one of her grandchildren equally, all for different reasons—my three children and my sister Amy's two, Sara and Andrew. Whether it was teaching Hilary to play the piano, sharing recipes with Whitney, engaging Michael in several

hands of cards, or hearing the latest reports from Sara and Andrew about their interests, Mom reveled in every interaction, and
each of them felt the same about time spent with her. And she never
tired of seeing Donna and her husband, David Rea, Amy and her
husband, David Peterson, B.J. and Krista, and me too.

In 2002, when Mom was diagnosed with cancer of the bile
ducts—cholangiocarcinoma—the doctors strongly recommended
surgery as the only treatment for this rare and aggressive form of
cancer. They let her know, however, that surgery was not a cure and
that the cancer could return. At eighty-three years old, Mom decided against having an operation. Based on what she had learned
from going through Dad's illness and death, and her own investiga-
tions, Mom felt that cutting near cancer could have the adverse
effect of causing it to spread. While she would continue visits to a
general practitioner to monitor her overall health, she more or less
chose to ignore what was growing inside her.

My siblings and I respected her decision but braced ourselves for
a speedy decline. We were told that with this kind of cancer, she
could be gone within a few months; at the most she might survive
for another year or so. We decided that for all those years that our
mother had put family first, we wanted and needed to put her first,
which meant coming together with a plan that would give her the
best quality of life for whatever time she had remaining. It was also
going to mean uprooting her.

Some years earlier, our romantic mother had decided it was time
to officially tie the knot with an adoring suitor who had been in her
life for only a short time. They ended up not actually living together,
mainly because neither wanted to give up the homes and the places

where they had spent most of their lives. Even so, they maintained their relationship in separate houses—an arrangement that turned out to be very healthy for Mom, who was always happier when there was a man in her life, whether or not they were under the same roof. At a certain point the house in Westernport had outgrown her, so she moved into a high-rise apartment building in nearby Keyser, West Virginia, that catered to seniors. Though she was farther away from her husband, she stayed close to her longtime friends and to the church and the community that had always been her rock of support.

Since all four of her children were living in and around the Baltimore area at the time, we decided the best plan would be to move her closer to us. When we told Mom that we wanted to move her down to my sister Amy's house—where we would congregate as often as possible—she embraced the plan immediately. The lesson we learned was that instead of devastating us, our family crisis with our mother's health gave us an opportunity to spend more time together as a family. Every weekend we gathered for meals and conversation, rallying around Mom in the process. Amazingly, after a while, she seemed to go into remission and declared that as much as she loved being with everyone, "I need my independence!"

Our next step was to find an assisted-living facility that would give her independence, her own social life, and access to medical and living assistance as needed. B.J.—the favorite son, the only son—worked hard canvassing area facilities and was able to locate a good place very close to where I was working. That way, I could stop off on a daily basis, before or after work—that is, as long as Mom could make time for me in her busy social schedule!

It was such a joy to share stories with her of the diverse, rich lessons that were revealed to me every day in my journey as an educator. After returning from Sydney, I had been energized in a variety of ways that would eventually carry over to the classroom and the schoolhouse. First of all, I was both humbled and proud to be among the family members of every athlete who had come to compete for the U.S. Olympic team. For years we had flown the colors of NBAC in competition, and I'd felt the same excitement whenever any of our club's swimmers won important races or set records, just as I could feel their disappointment and that of their family when expectations didn't pan out. Now we could feel the same passion to cheer for the home team, except that it had expanded to include everyone from across the United States. I knew there were millions of Americans back home watching on television—pinning their hopes on our champions representing us on the world stage. That same feeling of patriotism and connection that is part of the Olympic experience was something I wanted to share personally with my middle school students in Baltimore County—not as simply another sporting event but in a fashion that could be more meaningful and relevant to their lives. I wanted them to be able to share in the pride in our country and also to experience the Olympic spirit that connects us to citizens of other nations. I didn't know how to make those connections, but my creative wheels started to turn.

After five years and much success at Southwest Academy, by this time I had accepted an offer for what seemed like a position that would allow me to learn more in the arena of educational supervision and administration. The job was at Loch Raven Academy, which had three magnets—a well-established, high-achieving science magnet; a wonderful performing arts magnet with talented, motivated students; and a third promising but undeveloped magnet that I was coming in to spearhead. In these days, the old framework for teaching home economics had gone the way of rotary telephones and manual typewriters. The subject matter was often folded into other courses of study—not always for the better. When I was brought in to become the coordinator and administrative facilitator for this new magnet, which went under the catchall of health, finance, and law, I saw it as a fantastic opportunity to expand what we had accomplished at Southwest Academy and go further in teaching such vital life skills as financial and legal literacy, along with the fundamentals of personal and home health. Little did I know that this was the magnet for students who were considered low-achieving and were seen as less motivated—predominantly children of color and from minority backgrounds.

It certainly bothered me that expectations were set so low for our students, who, more than anything else, deserved our willingness to believe in them. As simple as that sounds, that turned out to be my greatest challenge—educating the younger, often intimidated teachers as well as the more mature but jaded staff, along with the rest of the system. My approach, rather than to lecture or preach, was to show what was possible and model the approach that I wanted other teachers to take.

There were two students in particular who several teachers had said were considered unruly and who lacked motivation. I thought that was nonsense! They happened to both be tall, big teens who had facial hair and were physically very mature compared to many other middle schoolers. They were also young men who needed

someone to recognize ways in which they could learn to be successful. One of them, it turned out, was gifted when it came to basketball and football; the other had a heart of gold and was a wonderful
writer, with deep dimples and charm for days. I took both young
men, along with all my students, under my wing and saw each of
them thrive more than anyone thought possible. In later years, I
was sorry to hear from their parents that their middle school experiences didn't prevent them from becoming involved in circumstances that led to incarceration. At the same time, the mother of
one of the young men let me know that after being released from
jail, he was able to implement many of the life skills he learned back
in middle school and put them toward becoming a successful and
great human being. Later, when I became an administrator, I kept
both of their stories and struggles in my heart—as reminders to
continue to be the idealist I am, as well as the realist who admits we
have more work to do.

More trials by fire came with my next position at Cockeysville
Middle School, a centralized summer school site, where I was appointed for a summer to serve as a glorified summer school
principal—with all the responsibilities and none of the perks. Just
as I was contemplating my next move, my mentor, Dr. Karen Roe,
alerted me that an amazing opportunity was going to be available
in the central office "on the hill," as we called the suite of buildings
housing the superintendent of Baltimore County and staff (along
with the executive directors of the different educational programs
and areas of our county, of which there were five).

In a restructuring move, the county's top-tier administrators
were going to be hiring five assistants to come in and work for the

executive directors who oversaw the various school branches—
elementary, middle, and high schools, along with alternative and
special needs schools. These five assistants were going to spend a
year learning everything about the school system and then play
coordinating roles in developing a comprehensive platform for the
next generation of top-achieving schools. This experience would
then lead to the next phase on their career path toward being a
school principal. Karen Roe insisted, "Debbie, this is a job for you.
It has your name all over it!"

Because the job announcement stated "select interview process,"
Karen wasn't sure if they actually had their five candidates in mind
or if I had a strong shot. Not only that, but the window was closing,
and I had to make sure my application was submitted right away.

When I followed up, sure enough, the deadline to apply was
approaching. By reorganizing several other priorities, I was fortunately able to submit my application on the last day before the
deadline. To my delight, and a bit to my surprise, I was selected for
an interview. Nonetheless, I knew there were possibly other candidates with more seniority within the Baltimore County Public
School system who were being considered. But as I headed to my
interview at the "big house" (as the superintendent's mansion on
the hill was known), I decided that this was going to be a learning
experience, no matter what—even though I didn't have any other
prospects on my horizon.

As I arrived for the appointment comfortably early, I did a last-
minute check of myself in a compact mirror to touch up my lipstick
and brighten my cheeks. There was a butterfly or two flutter kicking
inside me, I had to admit. Taking a deep breath, I thought, *C'mon,*

Debbie, you're almost fifty years old, you can do this! That didn't help until my thoughts flashed on all the years of watching Hilary, Whitney, and Michael show so much poise and confidence in situations where outcomes were totally unpredictable. That's all I needed to walk through the door and to give it all I had.

Inside there was a panel made up of the five executive directors in whose hands my fate (insofar as this job was concerned) would rest. A series of questions followed, most of which I was able to answer articulately and thoughtfully, or so I hoped. There was one indication that I had not done well, which came from a distinguished-looking gentleman who checked his wristwatch once or twice during my responses. *Oh, terrific,* I thought, *I'm really not impressing him!*

At the end of the interview, one of the other executive directors concluded with a last question, asking, "Ms. Phelps, if you don't get this job, what will your plans be for next year?"

"I will go back to the classroom."

"Does that bother you?"

"Not at all," I said with a smile. "Once a teacher, always a teacher."

A few days later, I received a phone call from one of the executive directors, Dr. Richard Milbourne, who wanted to let me know, "I'm going to put your name forth to the superintendent to fill the position for my assistant."

Dr. Milbourne was the one who had been glancing at his watch during the interview. That was simply who he was, a man who valued time and liked to be precise about it. He was also an exceptional, inspirational mentor with whom I would work closely for almost four years.

With that, I moved to the Greenwood central office on the hill, very close to my mother's assisted-living facility, and took on the title of assistant to the executive director of schools, Southwest. Together my mentor and I oversaw thirty-two schools in Baltimore County in a relationship that was tailor-made for our different styles. Dr. Milbourne's emphasis was on elementary grades, while I focused on secondary, yet we approached all our efforts as a partnership.

A southern gentleman who always called me Deborah, Dr. Milbourne demonstrated how he was able to move mountains in his quiet, behind-the-scenes way, yet also encouraged me to put my outgoing personality to use in most of our presentations and meetings. As a team, we had well-delineated roles suited to our respective areas of strength, with me always walking through the door first and him following, only one of his many habits that showed he was a true gentleman.

Every day was exiting, challenging, rewarding, and, as I often told my mother whenever I reviewed everything that was now being put on my plate personally and professionally, a learning experience for me. Dr. Milbourne was far ahead of his time in his willingness to embrace new strategies that were bearing fruit elsewhere and in his patience to plant seeds that might take time to produce measurable results. He was also not afraid to let go of practices that weren't working. As someone whose foundation was common sense, he was definitely a kindred spirit, a visionary. From the beginning, Dr. Milbourne's wonderful family—including his wife, Doris, and son, Richard, or "Ritchie"—embraced me and the members of my family in the most supportive, caring way.

Our team was comprised of the principals and staff at every schoolhouse in our jurisdiction. In addition to common sense, there was another *C* word that was all-important in these action-packed times: *composure*.

That was an attribute my mother had long epitomized and that I had valued in my teachers when I was growing up. It seemed to have added relevance for me not only as an administrator and educator but also as a mother, sister, daughter, and friend. Somewhere in the early 2000s, probably in '03, my mantra became "No worries." For the ability to maintain grace under fire and stay mostly unruffled even in the crazy whirlwind that by now had come to stay, I have to give partial credit to the tone set by Peter Carlisle and his team at Octagon.

Even though we'd been around the swimming world for years, and even though Bob Bowman had predicted just how far Michael's abilities could take him, nothing prepared any of us for the media onslaught that by this time, more than a year away from Athens, was already in full tilt. Michael managed to stay grounded in his sense of mission—to win that one Olympic gold medal, as he had determined—and to "keep it real," as one of my students had observed about him early on. He maintained his own form of composure in trying to balance high school, 365-day-a-year swim practice, and skyrocketing travel to international meets, together with his decision to go professional and handle the added pressure of corporate sponsorship. Initially, we thought it helped that Michael was able to get used to the attention on a local level as a hometown hero in Baltimore—to feel comfortable being in public, being himself. He stayed rooted in where he came from. But being in the public eye, even on the more local scale, would prove to be a double-edged sword. With greater attention, he would soon see, there would be even more perks and a more profound toll. Still, even the local media trap—the fishbowl—creates a stress factor all its own.

Michael and I developed a special signal for whenever these various stresses were getting to either of us. It started after a particular incident when he and Bob Bowman had a heated discussion about something or other. By the way, anyone who thinks that coaching Michael Phelps is the easiest job in sports is completely wrong. The funny thing is that while he may be naturally gifted athletically, it's ultimately the mental part of the game that determines victory or defeat. And that makes Michael one of the hardest athletes to coach—because he thinks for himself. Not only that, but as the ultimate competitor, he always wants to be right, even when he knows he isn't. Most of the time, no matter what the discussion was, Michael realized that Bob was right, but he would argue anyway just to assert his own authority and get a rise out of his coach, even taking pleasure in it sometimes. Bob knew this, but whenever he had reached his limit, it was Mom time.

So in the middle of this argument I happened to overhear, I gave Michael an emphatic look and pressed my hands in a downward motion to indicate that he should cool it. For a second he paused and stared at me strangely, as if to question whether I was trying a new dance move. Then I mouthed "Composure" and shot him the high C sign, putting my thumb and main forefinger together in the shape of a C. Like magic, it worked! He nodded, accepted the concept, and he and Bob went back to their strategy session just like that.

Well, maybe it wasn't *just* like that, but that's what I wanted to think.

Several months later I received a dose of my own medicine. That evening I was hustling around the kitchen, passing by the sink, washing a dish or two and preparing dinner in a decidedly stressed-out fashion. My "No worries" mantra was not cutting it for the amount of work that was piling up on my shoulders, plus everything that had to be done so that I could be ready to travel overseas, on top of concerns for how my mother was doing. I was thinking about Hilary's job, which was requiring her to travel much of the time, and about Whitney's starting a new job. With Michael set to graduate in spring 2003, it felt like everything was happening too quickly. I was feeling overwhelmed yet unable to put my finger on why.

It occurred to me as I was starting to have a meltdown that everyone has to hit their wall sometimes. Just as Hilary had hers in her teens when, exhausted from hours of training, she collapsed in my arms crying that morning after practice, Whitney reached her limit in her last year of college. It was then that she called me to say she wanted to leave the university and return home. Because she had such a short distance to go, I did everything in my power to convince her to stick with it until she got her degree. I reminded her how hard she had worked in her classes and how many obstacles she had overcome with her stellar, unbelievable determination. Why throw it away at the last minute? Of course, she knew I would be there to support her no matter what she decided, one hundred percent, but when she asked if I would provide her the means to move home, I said no. This was one of the few times I used that word, and it didn't go over well.

Whitney then reached out to Fred, who agreed to assist her financially so she could come home and move in with him and his wife—a situation to be short-lived. Even though Whitney and I went through an equally short-lived strain on our relationship, once we moved past it, we were closer than ever. As she set her sights on new passions to put her boundless energy and organizational skills to use in a career, opening up to her heart's desire to meet someone, fall in love, and start a family too, I was even more impressed with how she embarked on the next chapters of her life. Even so, whenever possible I did my best to plant a seed or two about returning to college one day to finish her degree.

So there I was, standing in the kitchen, thinking about the swift passing of the seasons and how my daughters were moving on. It began to dawn on me that perhaps, deep down, I was starting the natural mourning process that would occur when Michael moved out after high school. No sooner did I flash on the image of the empty nest but who should walk into the house through the kitchen door and come to a standstill? Michael. He took one look at me and said, "Mom, what's wrong?"

"Well," I began, "I just want everything to go smoothly and everyone to be okay and make sure you're ready . . . along with having dinner on the table for you thirty minutes after you get out of the pool from training because you need to eat," and before I could list everything that needed to be done or allow my tears to start falling, my favorite son, my only son, flashed me the C sign.

We both cracked up and gave each other well-deserved hugs.

With that, we kept on moving forward—one foot in front of the next, one lap after the other.

Around that time, as things became more and more hectic, the always cool, calm, collected, and composed team at Octagon introduced me to another much more applicable mantra. In the middle of a very nutty afternoon one Thursday toward the end of a school semester, one of the travel coordinators from Peter Carlisle's office asked how I was doing, really.

"Oh, fine," I answered.

"We have a policy that you can only be fine on Mondays," he joked. By Tuesday it was much too much to expect to be fine. By Wednesday, if you were still fine, you were in denial. Then again, he went on, "You do know what F.I.N.E. stands for, don't you?"

Apparently, it was an acronym:

F.I.N.E—Freaked out, Insecure, Neurotic, and Emotional

Except for "emotional," I decided all in one fell swoop that wasn't going to apply to me, so I stuck with the C word. That is, except for Mondays. From then on, I resolved to be fine only on Mondays.

Team Phelps had plenty of heart-pumping moments even before the Athens Olympic Games were upon us. The World Championships in Barcelona in July 2003 provided some of them. The trip there was definitely one of those experiences you can look back on and laugh about. At the time, the group of us who were traveling together—me, Hilary, B.J. and Krista, Gary Brewster, who had been Michael's high school government teacher, my cousin Darlene Blaney, along with other swim families—weren't laughing as we flew out of JFK Airport in New York. Our connecting flights on British Airways were subject to cancellation because the airline had just gone on strike while we were in the air.

We were supposed to fly on British Airways to Barcelona (through London), so we were understandably concerned. But we assumed that once we landed, the problem would be sorted out and we would just have to make our way to a ticket counter at another gate and book another flight. Much to our unhappiness, when we touched down in Heathrow, the scene was mayhem. Passengers were not only stranded but alternate forms of transportation were already tapped to the maximum, meaning people couldn't even leave the airport by taxis or buses.

It had been only a year and ten months since the terrorist attacks of 9/11, and the many intricacies of travel, as most of us know, had become more complicated due to security concerns. Our anxiety levels were duly heightened.

While figuring out a way to reroute wasn't hopeless, it was clearly not going to be quick or seamless. That added to the worries for some family members in our group, like the parents of Ed Moses, a 2000 Olympic medalist in the breaststroke, whose events were early in the competition. Sissy Moses, Ed's mom, was adamant that she not miss her son's races. "Make sure you're able to see your son swim at all times," she said to me. Her point was that as parents we should enjoy it while we could because the ride usually didn't last long.

Assistance finally came through after calls were made to the liaison for the U.S. swimming/parent organization that assists with travel for the parents as well as the athletes. We could thank Gary Brewster's extensive knowledge of international and governmental laws. We made our way to a section of the terminal where we seemed to be the only people left other than a few employees of British Airways who had been told to go and sit at their stations at the airport. One employee was a young fellow whose heartstrings we pulled—with true stories of our life savings being spent to see our family members swim in the World Championships—and who at last produced a piece of paper with information on it as to some possible assistance. With that in hand, and instructed by the U.S. swimming parent liaison not to leave the airport, we found another possible connection at another terminal, so we hurried downstairs to grab our luggage and run.

As we arrived at what should have been our baggage carousel, we saw thousands and thousands of bags littering the floor, covering every inch of usable space. I'd never seen so many black suitcases in my life. With Gary's family background in public service and his own talents for systemizing, he took charge and devised a plan for finding our luggage, then for making it to the other terminal in time to get on our flight to Barcelona or thereabouts. From the fire to the frying pan, we left the abandoned terminal and arrived at the other one, which was also overflowing with hot, sweaty, and fed-up travelers. Some of the men were shirtless, apparently acceptable in European culture but not so pleasant in those crowded conditions. Herded pretty much like cattle through narrow quarters with low ceilings, we learned that we would have to wait in line with our bags in order to purchase tickets.

Once again, Gary Brewster marshaled our forces to make sure we posted representatives in every line we could find. Hilary, amazing navigator that she is, was also in the lead, helping to ensure that information flowed to one and all in our group as she used her signature cheer and people talents to help keep spirits up. Ironically, no one spoke English at these various other airline counters, even though we were in England. We were strangers in a strange land.

Miraculously, we all made it onto a flight—with not one seat or second to spare. The only hitch was that it was not going to Barcelona but to Paris. We'd left JFK on a Friday, and when we arrived in France, it was Saturday night, and Charles de Gaulle Airport was pretty much closed. We were told to leave and come back the next day.

"Non, merci," we replied, we were staying put and sleeping at the airport so we could be on the earliest flight to Barcelona. We all did our best to find seats to sleep on, wearing the same clothes we'd been wearing since the day before, using our luggage and pocketbooks for pillows. At around the same time that night, in Barcelona, Michael had contacted Candy, our point person/parent liaison at USA Swimming, who had helped so much in procuring our tickets, to say he wanted to go see his family at their hotel.

Candy didn't want to worry him about our being stuck in Paris and sleeping in the airport, so she told him it was too late to call or go to the hotel and that his family would see him at the pool the next day. Score another one for composure!

Finally, on Sunday, we arrived in Barcelona and went straight to the pool without changing. Fortunately, all the swimmers were able to see their family members in the stands, waving and cheering as if nothing had happened.

The buzz in Barcelona—stirred up mostly by the Australian media—was the controversy over why so much attention was being given to upstart Michael Phelps, an eighteen-year-old who, they repeatedly pointed out in articles and broadcasts, had only come in fifth in one event in Sydney; they downplayed his accomplishments since then. The Australian journalists mostly wanted to scoff at the idea that he was a contender for the throne of Ian Thorpe, their national hero, who at that time was considered to be the greatest swimmer in the world.

Michael didn't let any of this "parking-lot gossip" (as we had called it at NBAC) get to him. If anything, he used it for motivation—winning gold in the 200-meter butterfly (breaking his own world record), golds in both the 200-meter individual medley and the 400-meter individual medley (setting world records in each), and sharing gold for the 4×100 relay, winning silver in the 100-meter butterfly and another silver for the 4×200 relay (an American record). These accomplishments put an end to any idea that Michael was receiving undue hype. After that, Michael said his new mantra was the age-old powerful truth "Actions speak louder than words."

I felt bad when, just to demonstrate how fickle fans and media can be, some Aussie journalists started to criticize Thorpe's performance and question whether his star had ceased to rise. In that atmosphere, I had a chance to meet Ian Thorpe's mom, who was doing her best to retain grace under fire. Without specifically talking about it, she gave me a sense of what it must be like to have a son who couldn't walk down the street without being mobbed. She exuded the same mix of emotions that would become more familiar to me—the same motherly pride combined with a desire to protect your loved one from relentless public scrutiny and the demands on time and privacy. After all, no matter how superhuman the feats of Olympians on track and field, in the gym and the pool, they are still very much human.

Interestingly enough, I learned in Barcelona that Ian's mother was an educator and his older sister had been a world-class swimmer who had competed at the Pan Pacific championships the same year Whitney had been there. Small world, indeed.

When Mrs. Thorpe and I met in Barcelona, gracious as she was, I could tell she wasn't pleased about all the talk of a rivalry between Ian and Michael. To me, the desire to compete against your role model and inspiration was a form of flattery—a sign of admiration and respect. When asked about the rivalry, however, and her thoughts on the matter, Mrs. Thorpe said something along the lines of "My son has no rival."

That may have been true when it came to the 200-meter freestyle—the only event in which Michael would have an opportunity to swim against Ian Thorpe in Athens. Other attempts by Michael to pursue or create marquee competitions between the two of them went forward but were never realized, usually because Ian declined or was otherwise obligated. So, to create added motivation, pressure, and drama, Michael, Bob, and Peter Carlisle took advantage of a marketing strategy that Speedo could seize upon that referenced an icon and his historic legacy—Mark Spitz and the seven gold medals he'd won in one Olympic Games in 1972.

When I heard about it and the deal that Speedo made to award one million dollars to Michael if he broke the record and won eight gold medals, I thought it was brilliant.

Without question, the buzz it stirred was going to add immeasurable pressure to a swimmer whose main goal was to win just one gold medal. But my attitude at first was that it was a no-lose proposition. If he didn't win all eight golds to break Spitz's record, he was still certain to have an amazing showing. As Michael kept reminding everyone, as long as he went forward to swim his best time and enjoy himself, that was what mattered. That's not to say that the goal of surpassing Mark Spitz in the history books was all pie in the sky. After all, records are made to be broken.

The downside to the whole gamble was the media obsession it would become. Another lesson coming right up.

In the meantime, Leoma Davisson—who probably knew more about Mark Spitz than I ever did, or Michael for that matter—was as excited as most of the media about how high her grandson had set the bar for himself. I'll never forget how she reacted one day when there was a group of family members visiting her and Michael showed up to surprise her.

Thinking that Gran would be delighted to see him, Michael was taken aback when she looked at him and asked, "What are you doing here? You should be at practice." Mom wasn't kidding.

Michael tried to explain that it had taken a lot of effort to come to see her. And that there was "tapering" between major meets, meaning that swimmers lightened their practice hours to rest their bodies in order to give them extra energy reserves when it counted. But Gran wasn't hearing any of it. Banished, Michael promised her that he was ready for Olympic trials and for the games, if that was in the cards.

I t was right about that time, in the midst of all this momentum, that I came to an unexpected turning point in my career. I was summoned to the office of the superintendent of schools in Baltimore County, Dr. Joe A. Hairston. By this era, I was well established in my role as an administrative facilitator and couldn't imagine being happier than I was working with Dr. Milbourne. It was the next best thing to what I considered my true dream job: being made principal of my own schoolhouse.

My closest allies knew that and were in my corner, cheering for me. The question was, when I was called in to see the superintendent, was he in agreement?

There aren't enough words to express my admiration for Dr. Hairston, lovingly known to his principals as Dr. Joe. He had taken his post in 2000 as the first African American superintendent of Baltimore County's public schools and had swiftly become a national spokesperson and leader with amazing results. When he called me in, of course I hoped there was good news in the offing, as opposed to all the other scenarios that might have crossed my mind. But in any case, whatever it was, this was not to be a discussion. Whether I was being given a promotion or the opposite, I knew there was only one answer: "Yes, sir. On behalf of the school system, I'll be happy to serve."

So I walked out of our offices and up the brick walkway and entered the stately mansion where the superintendent has his office. As soon as I arrived, Dr. Hairston stood and smiled, greeted me, and waited for me to sit down before he said, "Debbie, I'm appointing you principal of Woodland Middle School." Before I could react with euphoria, he added, "You'll report on July first."

I looked back at him, saying nothing, waiting for the reality to hit. He had just told me he wanted me to have my own schoolhouse. It was a low-performing middle school with a predominantly African American student body, right on the city/county line. And I would need to report on July 1.

"Thank you very much, sir," I said. "It's a great honor." Then I took a deep breath as I continued, "I know I can do that job and I am honored that you believe in me. But I can't accept."

His eyes widened as he asked, "What do you mean?"

"I mean, I have the confidence that I can do the job." I paused, searching for the diplomatic way to say that I wouldn't be able to do the job as it needed to be done right now. "Well, you see, you have a low-performing school and, here's the thing, sir, I have the 2004 Olympic trials in Long Beach and hopefully the Olympic Games in Athens, and I believe my son is going to make history of some sort, and I need to be there. This is Michael's summer."

Dr. Hairston scrutinized me as he said drily, "Both of my sons played football, and I made it to all of their games when I was an administrator."

"I'm not going to be available in July," I countered, pointing out that that was when the new principal needed to be on duty. "I'm going to be in Long Beach at trials."

"You have an experienced, strong administrative team," Dr. Hairston argued, letting me know it would be acceptable to let my staff open the school year for me until I returned in the fall.

"I don't care how strong an administrative team there is, you are assigning white Debbie Phelps to a predominantly African American school, and if you want me to give one hundred percent to that school, to build the relationships that will be vital to the work ahead, I have to be there 24-7 plus, every day of this summer. I need to be visiting their churches, meeting with business and community groups, establishing a rapport long before the doors to the schoolhouse open in the fall. I need to have the families of that community find out who I am, what I am about, how we can work together, and how they can trust me."

Dr. Hairston just looked at me thoughtfully and, after several seconds of silence, nodded his head and said, "You go to Athens, Debbie, and when you come back, we'll talk."

With that I stood up and said, "Thank you, sir," and I left his office knowing that most likely I was not going to be principal of Woodland Middle School, but not really knowing where I was going to be when I returned from Athens. Out of work? Heading back to the classroom? It would be a couple of months before I would know the answer and another year before the final verdict would come in. But in the meantime, I knew that whatever the outcome, the risk taken would be worth it.

From start to finish, everything about the 2004 Olympic Games in Athens was just about perfect. And no matter how many times I've relived the highlights of it—from the ultimate DP moment when Michael pushed his first-ever gold medal through the fence for me and his sisters to touch, saying, "Look what I did," through all eight medals he won in total—the memories would only become more cherished with the years.

True, he won only six gold medals; the other two were bronze. No, he didn't top the record of Mark Spitz or win his deal from Speedo. But that only gave him a higher mountain to climb. And what he had already done was to shatter a multitude of other records, starting at the Olympic trials in Long Beach when he became the first swimmer ever to qualify for six individual events, and then in Athens for that first race, the 400-meter individual medley, when he won in world-record time—ahead of the rest of the field by three and a half seconds. If he had stopped with one gold medal, that would have been history-making on its own, but then he went on to win five more—in the 200-meter butterfly, the 100-meter butterfly, in the 200-meter individual medley, and as part of the teams that won the 4×200-meter freestyle relay and the 4×100-meter medley relay.

Though I believed that the bronze he and Team USA won for the 4×100-meter freestyle relay would provide motivational fodder for upcoming competitions, Michael felt emotionally exhausted after that hard-battled race. The upset was less about missing a shot at breaking the Spitz record and more, I believed, about Michael hating to let his teammates down.

One of the most admirable traits that Michael exhibited in these Games (and continues to demonstrate) is that whenever he has the opportunity to credit someone else for their contribution, he will; whenever there is a shortcoming or a falter, whether or not he's really to blame, he'll take responsibility for it. What a magnificent way to represent your family, your city and state, your nation, and the Olympic ideal. How could I have asked for anything more? Hilary and Whitney felt the same pride in those attributes that I did as a mom. Then there was his speed in the water. Amazing.

The day after the third-place showing in the 4×100 freestyle relay, with that sober expression still on his face, Michael walked out onto the pool deck to compete in the 200-meter freestyle—against not only Ian Thorpe but also Pieter van den Hoogenband of the Netherlands (the defending Olympic gold medalist who had upset Thorpe in this event four years earlier) and Australia's Grant Hackett, who was considered to be the dark horse. Much of the murmuring in the media gave props to Michael for taking the gamble on an event that he wasn't established in—especially because he went into the race with his only opportunity to equal the gold medal record of Mark Spitz. But it was also his only opportunity to race against Ian Thorpe—a hero and a rival—and Michael didn't want to miss that chance. After a memorably slow start off the blocks, Michael put tremendous pressure on van den Hoogenband and Thorpe but couldn't catch up until the last 50 meters, when the Phelps closing power kicked in. His ability to accelerate dramatically in the closing seconds like that caused many observers to say that Michael would have won gold if there had simply been a little bit more pool. As it was, Ian Thorpe reclaimed some history for himself and won the gold medal, with van den Hoogenband touching next for silver and leaving the bronze for Michael.

While that was a momentary letdown for Team Phelps, I was in awe of what I had witnessed. Ian Thorpe would retire shortly after these Games, but even without Michael's winning a race against him, there was no doubt that the torch had been passed. Therefore, I was stunned when a member of the European press approached me to find out how devastated I was over Michael's not surpassing or matching the Mark Spitz record. "Tonight," he said, "the world has moved on and left your son behind."

Even though I wanted to say, "What Olympics have you been watching, mister?" I retained my composure and said, "My son has written a page of history and there will be more to come, not only from my son but the entire U.S. Olympic team. He is only halfway through the Olympic program for this Olympics."

Michael answered critics who said he had failed to become the next Mark Spitz by letting them know he was never interested in being the next anybody else. He was focused on being the first Michael Phelps. Even though he hadn't met the goal—yet—of breaking the Spitz record, he had drawn more and new attention to the sport of swimming. And that was only the beginning.

One of the few notes of discord that I recall in the entire '04 Olympics experience came from comments Fred had made to Michael before the games about security concerns. Certainly, in a post-9/11 world everyone had to abide by much greater security measures than in the past. Moreover, there was the history of terrorism at the 1972 Munich Olympics. That made the purpose of the Olympic Games as a time for all nations to come together in peace and goodwill all the more meaningful. It was also a time for Americans at home in a time of war to see our flag embraced and admired by the rest of the world and to honor our men and women in uniform who were committing their lives to protect and defend our citizens. That's why our Olympians were all exemplary every time any of them was asked about security concerns; all expressed their confidence in the Greek and Olympic authorities for every security measure implemented. The message sent was one of strength, courage, and resilience.

As the Games were coming to a close and our stay in Athens was slowly ending, Hilary, Whitney, and I attended a party at a lovely apartment in the valley along the mountain's edge that bordered the ancient city—a beautiful setting. The party coincided with what was supposed to be Michael's last swim—the 4×100 medley relay—but this being one of the few opportunities to socialize with Greek hosts and fellow family members of Olympians, we accepted the invitation. Just as we were entering, our phone rang and Hilary answered. A friend from NBC called to inform us of the latest AP wire story saying that Michael Phelps had relinquished his spot in the finals to Ian Crocker. Since Michael had helped his team qualify by swimming earlier on the B team, he would still be eligible to win the medal whether he swam in the finals or not. Ian, a 2000 gold medalist who had lost in Athens to Michael by .04 seconds in the 100-meter butterfly, had not been feeling well earlier in the Games but had rallied in time for the final swim. By pulling out, Michael was giving Ian an opportunity to compete and medal—a win-win since the swimmers on the team that qualified in the preliminaries would medal too.

It was a generous and sportsmanlike gesture on Michael's part, on the one hand. On the other, I had to warm up to the idea. After all, this was Athens—the home of the Olympics—where tradition had ruled since ancient times. To abide by that tradition meant so much; Michael would be swimming in the first of the swim events and then in the last of them, at the opening and the closing. I confess I also wanted him to be part of the four to swim to gold against the Australians.

But by the time I had a chance to mull it over, I was that much prouder of Michael's decision. When I told him so, he was modest about it, saying, "Ian deserved to swim that race." The gold medal that was scored allowed Ian Crocker to medal and share in the glory. And by adding that eighth medal to his count, Michael made a bit more history by becoming the second athlete ever to win a total of eight medals in a single Olympics.

We arrived home to a hero's welcome that was truly the stuff of which dreams are made. It seemed that most of Baltimore and Maryland turned out for a combination parade and festival. It was being billed as a Phelpstival with presentations by a host of distinguished officials including the governor and Dr. Joe A. Hairston.

Before Michael had flown in to enjoy his celebration and to learn that the street in front of Towson High School had been renamed Michael Phelps Way, I had happily learned from Dr. Joe that I would be remaining in the same job on the hill for the 2004/05 school year. I was looking forward to immersing myself in the work ahead, knowing that I would need the structure more than ever now with the empty nest that I was going to be facing, whether I was ready or not.

Before Olympic trials, Bob Bowman was made an offer he couldn't turn down to coach at the University of Michigan—a top swimming school. The Wolverines baseball hat that Michael had been wearing for years because he was a fan must have been some kind of omen. In any case, I wasn't surprised by Michael's decision to attend college in Ann Arbor, where Bob was headed. Four years to Beijing for the 2008 Olympics sounded like a long time, but I knew better.

With the logistics as complicated as they were, it turned out that Michael was only flying in for his events and not even staying at home before leaving again on a thirteen-city tour. For the first time as his mother, I was dealing with the typical nineteen-year-old who forgets to call home, only I had the Internet and the TV showing me where he was turning up, almost like a *Where's Waldo?* of my son, leading me to coin the expression "Where in the world is Michael Phelps?" When the tour culminated at Disney World, I went there for part of the festivities and we had a few minutes to talk.

Now I started to worry. Especially after hugging him and asking, "How are you?" and hearing his answer, "My back hurts. And I am tired."

When I urged him to make sure to take care of himself, he said the only thing he had planned was to buy himself a new car. He also wanted to rekindle old friendships and hang out with those friends. Then he would be off to Ann Arbor to settle in for classes and get back to the pool.

I told him, "No worries," and promised to pack his bedroom for him and to have the boxes ready when the moving company came to get them.

I figured I could use the project to decompress after all the excitement. But, life being what it is, there were other issues to consider. When I visited Mom not long after the post-Olympics fanfare had quieted down, I knew she was not long for this world. As summer turned to fall, I watched her take a turn for the worse. She was eighty-five years old—with more life, wisdom, joy, and love packed into those years than could ever be measured—but her time was coming to an end. I wasn't ready to say good-bye. Not that you are ever ready for loss.

Nor was I ready for the call from a reporter that came in on my phone one day, about six weeks after the Olympics, when I happened to be at a schoolhouse doing an on-site event.

Phone calls from media weren't that unusual since almost every television channel in Baltimore knew they could talk to me. Sometimes I would route them to Peter Carlisle for national interviews, but there was a comfort level with most local outlets. This reporter had decided to contact me for a comment on the story that had not yet broken about the arrest of Michael Phelps for driving under the influence.

When my senses got past the shock, and I realized he was talking about my Michael Phelps, I said nothing to indicate I had no idea what he meant and stated that he needed to call Octagon. After a series of furious, tearful phone calls, I learned that the previous night Michael had been arrested down at the shore—on a DUI in which he was driving his new Range Rover with friends in it and almost caused a terrible accident, but didn't. Michael had called Peter the previous night. I expected that after a state trooper made the arrest, Fred would have been notified. But he received the news the same day that I did.

In the meantime no one knew what the press reaction was going to be or when it would hit.

Still in a state of disbelief, I drove to the lawyer's office, where I saw Michael. His face was immensely, profoundly sad and clearly very sorry. He later acknowledged that the sight of my face was dev-astating. "I never want to see my mom looking at me that way again" was what he told more than a few people. Nothing like this had ever happened with him. It was unreal.

The first person I called was B.J., and I asked him to make phone calls for me, as I was bracing myself for the deluge.

My first priority was that he call our mother. Coming from her favorite son/only son, the news would, I hoped, be less devastating to her. B.J. also called Hilary and Whitney to tell them not only what had happened but why I wasn't staying at home. After that, I had to call my boss so he knew and could notify the superintendent.

When the news broke, it spread like wildfire, like something out of a horror movie—with TV clips of jail cell doors slamming omi-nously shut, dooming the life and career of one golden boy turned loser. In a matter of a couple of months since Athens, the entire parking-lot gossip machine turned viciously from building this nineteen-year-old boy up to the skies to slamming him down.

While I stayed at the home of friends, Hilary and Whitney had to go in stealth, in the dark of night, to my back door so that they could slip inside and collect clothes and toiletries for me. The two of them couldn't even turn on lights inside for fear of alerting the reporters who were camped out on my lawn.

During the furor, I blamed myself, not that I should have. But I was sure I could have done something to better prepare Michael to make better choices. Peter Carlisle was a pillar of support, remind-ing me throughout the process, "I know this is really hard on you, but it will not last. Michael will do the right thing, and the media cycle will run its course." Bob Bowman was pretty crushed too but saw the big picture and reinforced Peter's message that "this too shall pass." Hilary and Whitney stayed very close during the ordeal, hurting for me as well as for Michael.

As I learned more of the details of the incident, I blamed him less because he had actually tried to have someone else drive after he'd had a few drinks. Apparently someone in the crowd had made a crack about not giving the keys to his brand-new Range Rover to someone else. Michael never blamed that person but took full responsibility, putting in more hours of community service than required—working with Mothers Against Drunk Driving and then speaking to Boys & Girls Clubs about making better choices. He also behaved with remorse and dignity when he appeared in court, while the media circus was excessive during the public hearing when he went in front of a judge to plead guilty and express just how sorry he was.

Michael was clearly mortified but never really buckled until one point later on when we were going through Penn Station in New York for a Golden Goggles event and a kid called to him, "Hey, Phelps!" Michael turned with a smile, as if to say hello, only to hear, "Let's go have a beer." The look on his face then was so sad. When we arrived at the hotel, Hilary noticed Michael resting his head in his hands, still haunted by that comment.

It took me almost a week to go back to work. During that time, I stayed out of sight, hibernating at a friend's house, crying my eyes out. I'd never missed a day's work in my working life; with all the ups and downs, I'd managed to show up on time, straight from the airport if need be, but always there. Well, that was a record that was broken. I now let myself mourn many years' worth of pent-up stuff, allowing myself to be freaked out, insecure, neurotic, and emotional (F.I.N.E.) for more than one day.

From the time that my father died, I had been the DP version of the unsinkable Molly Brown, never stopping to mourn losses or to have regrets. Enough was enough. I cried about the divorce, about the disappointments, about whatever I needed to cry about. All that time of being strong and just stepping one foot in front of the next, I had never cried uncle. And now I could do that.

After that week, true to Peter's prediction, the media cycle ran its course and the public moved on. I went back to work, no worse for wear. That was, until the day when I had to face the movers who arrived to pick up all the boxes for Michael. I then spent some more days grieving that my little boy, my now young man, had gone off to college.

As hard as that time was, it taught me a lesson long overdue. Just as all my favorite people in the world were only human—including the lights of my life, Hilary, Whitney, and Michael—it finally dawned on me that I was too. Hallelujah.

ELEVEN

The Platform Unfolds

As my three siblings would join me in attesting, the mold was absolutely broken when our mother came into this world in 1919. Leoma Foote Davisson took everything life handed to her—the gifts, the burdens, the joys, and the sorrows—and made the most of every second of her existence. She lived every moment on her own terms, like no one else I've ever known. In the words of her grandchildren, she was truly "awesome."

It shouldn't have been a surprise that she would leave nothing to chance when it came to how she was going to die. Strange as that sounds, from the time the doctors at Johns Hopkins gave her a grim prognosis, she made up her mind that she would do it all her way.

Though I knew she would want to chime in on how she would ultimately go to her final resting place, I remember thinking it was somewhat freaky when the cancer was first diagnosed and she went home to what she fondly called her "high-rise" apartment—where she was still living then—and sat down to create the master plan we were expected to follow. But that's who she was, a woman who liked things done a certain way—not unlike yours truly and a few other Davissons and Phelpses I know.

Mom not only decided to be cremated but also wrote her own obituary and told us which photograph she wanted to be placed in the newspaper, as well as which photographs should be on display at the funeral. Even before we moved her down to Baltimore to live closer to us, she made sure all the arrangements had been discussed with the funeral home in Westernport, as well as with our church. When B.J. and I went to leave the deposit at the funeral home, we selected everything according to Mom's wishes—the right urn, the style for how the program should be printed, and even which note cards we would be using to write thank-yous for condolences and flowers. Then we returned and had lunch with her to review our selections. Everything was in order.

Never underestimate the power of a plan if you want to achieve lofty goals. Once she had these arrangements in place and knew they would be handled properly later on, Gran applied her odds-defying talents to living almost three years beyond the best estimate she was given. However, in the winter following the Olympics in Athens, as we all came down from that unbelievable high, it was almost as if her defenses finally gave in and her body didn't have the same fight any longer. At that point she was given hospice care at the assisted-living facility, care that was phenomenal. I will never forget how lovingly she was treated by the medical and caregiving staff.

Mom then set a new goal for herself, informing all of us that winter, "I want to live to be eighty-six." She explained, "I just don't want to die at eighty-five."

I don't know why I thought that was so ambitious. But sure enough, as the calendar year flipped another page, Mom remained with us, determined to last all the way to Thanksgiving. During those months, though it was heartbreaking to see her struggle physically, I cherished our visits, even though, with every one, I thought it could be our last.

But as I'd wipe my eyes, heading down the hallway, thinking I'd never see her again, the nurses would always reassure me, "Come back tomorrow to see your mother. She'll be here."

In her later years, Mom gained a reputation in our family for being blunt in the way she dispensed advice. When she saw me suffer so much in the wake of Michael's DUI, she really helped me put that into perspective and into context. She didn't say, "Debbie, just get over it and stop blaming yourself." Mom did acknowledge how upsetting it all was. As a parent, you have to do that. But she also pointed out, "We learn from mistakes and we can still celebrate successes." It was all part of growth. Then her focus was on how to move forward.

Gran's balanced way of looking at the situation helped me begin to realize that in many ways, the whole thing had been a blessing in disguise—one of those teachable moments for Michael. The experience enabled him to learn how much scrutiny he was going to face and how his actions outside the pool would have consequences, as they should. Nobody likes to hear that you learn more from your mistakes than from moments of triumph, but it's often true.

During my one-on-one visits with Mom, I was able to share all the exciting news in the works—especially the upcoming wedding of Whitney Phelps to Bob Flickinger, the loving, handsome, intelligent, and wonderfully down-to-earth man to whom she was engaged. Gran was able to hear Whitney tell her all about the plan that was unfolding for this joyful occasion.

Both my daughters visited Gran almost on a weekly basis, and while it was hard on the two of them to watch the suffering of this tenacious, effervescent lady they both adored, the three of them never seemed to run out of things to talk about. Mom loved hearing about her granddaughters' love lives—she was a romantic to the end—and she kept up her telephone conversations with her boyfriend back in Keyser. At almost eighty-six years old, she still stressed to Hilary and Whitney the gift of true love, how she'd given up her scholarship to Peabody to study music so she could marry their grandfather Beau.

Love was what mattered most, Gran believed—the family framework. Interestingly enough, her advice was different with each of her grandchildren. With Michael, she didn't want him to get tied down too young; she used to tell him to date as much as he could before getting serious. She would say, "Love them all, Michael, you know, *spread* the love."

While Mom was delighted that Whitney had met the right person, her message to Hilary was to listen to her own heart and not be in a rush for marriage. She told her that instead she should pursue her career with all the passion she had for it. Gran insisted, "Don't be in a hurry to settle down. I want you to wait until you're sure you've met the love of your life. You deserve the absolute best!"

Then there was another lecture Mom tried to give me whenever the topic arose of why I wasn't dating. "Debbie," she said to me on a regular basis, "you need a boyfriend, a man."

"I have no time, Mom," I'd quip, hoping not to go any further with a discussion about why I was married to my job and was being "too picky," according to her. More than once she tried to talk about the importance of male companionship at her age as well as mine, at which point I would blush.

"Mom!" I'd say, "do we really have to talk about this?"

"I'm just telling it like it is."

"I know, but you're my mother."

"Oh, Debbie, lighten up," she'd say with a laugh. "You're so English." There it was again, the way she described me for being too prim. "You really should have a man in your life."

I settled it by saying, "When it's meant to be, I fully believe the right man will come along."

Mom was adamant that nothing in life just happened spontaneously or magically when "it was meant to be." Goals had to be set; plans had to be made.

That was exactly what had been in her thinking before she passed away on November 29, 2005—days after Thanksgiving. She was eighty-six years old, which had been her goal and her plan. The last time I visited her, I thought Mom might make it to eighty-seven. But the nurses knew. This time, when I said, "See you tomorrow," they nodded a bit uncertainly but echoed my words anyway, saying, "See you tomorrow too."

Donna, Amy, B.J., and I returned to Westernport to do our utmost in seeing that every detail for the funeral was handled in exactly the way Mom had intended. Michael, Hilary, and Whitney met in Baltimore and decided to caravan in separate cars to the funeral. As competitive as the three are, they couldn't agree about who should lead, and each kept trying to pass the other two all the way there. Thankfully, some things don't change.

Donna's husband, David Rea, now a retired Baptist minister, was able to serve, as he did lovingly, as the minister for the memorial service that was held at the funeral home. After he finished the eulogy, he asked if anyone would like to speak, and the first person to quickly rise to his feet, walk to the front, and turn to the packed crowd of mourners who had come to pay their respects—friends, members of our church, Mom's colleagues from school, and even some of our schoolteachers—was Michael. He didn't hold back from letting his tears fall in remembering how much he loved Gran. Michael reminisced about how she taught him to play all those games—500 rummy, hearts, and kings in the corner—and how she was as competitive as he was, accusing him of cheating whenever she didn't win.

Michael spoke about what an important influence she had been in his life and recalled the time when he was preparing to buy his very first car and Gran only had one piece of advice: "Buy a Cadillac." She believed a Cadillac was the kind of car that makes a real statement about who you are—and that it would suit him very well.

Against all kinds of other advice, Michael's first car was indeed a Cadillac—a custom Escalade SUV with tinted windows and spinning rims that were very popular at the time. It might not have been what Gran had visualized exactly, but it was a Cadillac nonetheless.

Sitting there watching Michael speak, I flashed on many earlier scenes of Gran interacting with him and his sisters at so many stages of their development. Hilary and Whitney opted not to speak, perhaps owing to their emotion or a feeling that their brother had represented them in his remarks. Yet I was so grateful that the three had been there for her, each in their own way, just as Gran had been there for them, never forgetting a birthday or a holiday, simply reminding them how happy it made her to watch them grow and find their way in the world, through better and worse, ups and downs—a grandmother for all seasons.

Looking around at our family, I felt enormous pride for the matriarch whom we were honoring and whom we would miss so much. In the midst of grief, I found a sense of peace and gratitude for the richness of Mom's life that in turn created life for Donna, Amy, B.J., and me—and for the five grandchildren who were continuing this vital, loving, strong family tree, as well as for our next generation to come. What a legacy—family!

After I rose to speak and to share my appreciation for everything Mom had taught me about being a lady and carrying myself with grace and poise, and after remembrances that were shared by others after me, I had a chance to exchange embraces with many friends I hadn't seen in decades. That helped me prepare for the good-bye that came at the cemetery, where Mom's ashes were interred in a grave next to my father's. Just as we all were turning to go, Michael went over to the man who was overseeing this process that had been so carefully planned by Leoma. Michael handed the man a few items to be buried along with Gran's ashes—a couple of playing cards from a deck they must have used in a memorable game of hearts, and just to make sure she would know it was from him, a pair of his winning swim goggles.

In the midst of sorrow and loss, other more welcomed seasons were beginning for all of us, as we came together for an unforgettable celebration—Whitney's wedding. Not surprisingly, Whitney was fully in charge of the wedding plans in the weeks leading up to the big day for her and Bob. Everything about it promised to be absolutely exquisite—from the gorgeous setting at Bob's parents' house near Rockville, Maryland, not far from Washington, D.C., with beautiful landscaping complete with a pond, a multitiered deck, and a stone patio. Whitney's vision for the ceremony was to use the winding brick pathway that wove in and out of the trees as the aisle leading up to where my brother-in-law, David Rea, Donna's husband, would be in charge of officiating. Afterward, the reception was to be held in a big tent with the interior adorned by hundreds of tiny white lights and autumn flowers, and everything shimmering with hanging Chinese lanterns, arrangements full of the delicate berry branches known as bittersweet, thin white silver dollar pods on strands amid more flowers—right out of a storybook.

Bob's mother, Cathy, and I hit it off from the moment we were introduced as future in-laws. We laughingly decided that she was the blond version of me and I was the brunette version of her. Whitney may have been in charge of all decisions, but Cathy and I were there to collaborate and help her pull it all off—just as my mother had helped me during my wedding. As much as I love helping throw all parties and celebrations, this was the most fun I'd experienced in years—which was exactly what I told Whitney when I arrived for the weekend to stay with the Flickingers and started work hanging the Chinese lanterns.

From start to finish, I could not have been a prouder mother of the bride. Watching Whitney take charge and make decisions at a level that I'd never seen before was such a testament to how much she had healed from earlier disappointments. It was also moving to see how she and Bob shared the same values and how they made choices to honor family first and foremost. On Friday night, they decided that we were going to have the rehearsal at the Flickingers' house so we could continue preparing for the wedding the next day. We weren't going to do anything elaborate for the rehearsal other than review the order of the ceremony and who would do what, as is traditional, and then afterward have dinner at the country club where Bob's parents, Cathy and John, were members.

It was during the rehearsal that I had the occasion to look up and see a most touching image I will always treasure. By that point, Michael had arrived and was pitching in on the preparations as well.

After he had first walked in—somewhat late, because his flight had been delayed—the first thing Michael did was to come and give me a hug and a kiss, and then he did the same with Hilary and Whitney, before turning to Bob to give him a pat on the back and a handshake. No doubt he was joking around to calm the groom's nerves. My eyes misted over when I saw that gesture, which let me know that Michael really viewed his new brother-in-law as a member of the family. It was also clear that he was aware how much this was a rite of passage for Whitney—just as we had celebrated when Hilary graduated from the University of Richmond and had cheered him on in Athens. Now it was Whitney's turn.

A short while later, as the rehearsal continued, the emotion of what we had been through as a family—the amazing ups and some serious downs over the past years—took hold of my three children as they spontaneously came together in a sight I will never forget. From my seat in the front where the mother of the bride traditionally sits, I looked up at one point and glanced over at Whitney and saw how Michael and Hilary each had their arms around her, the three of them just standing there as one, holding each other up, letting Whitney be as emotional as she chose to be, no one saying a word.

The only image that could compete with that one was during the wedding itself the next day when I beheld the scene of Michael beaming as he stood next to his sisters, Hilary as maid of honor, looking on, and Whitney holding hands with Bob, my new son-in-law, gazing at his bride as if to say that he was the luckiest guy in the world—all in all, a storybook wedding.

As a parent, one of the most gratifying experiences is to know that you have nurtured all of your children and that they are one another's number one cheerleaders. That was certainly the case with how my mother and father raised me and my siblings; now the torch had been passed. The unconditional love and support that Hilary, Whitney, and Michael have for one another is beautiful to see. Their resilience as individuals and as members of Team Phelps was inspiring to me too. Indeed, as I reflected on the events of the past year and thought about what could have stalled me way back then, I could take heart in seeing that it had been overcome and that my journey had moved on in extraordinary ways. As it so happened, this time period marked a new beginning for me with an ambitious platform I'd been building for the last two and a half years that was unfolding in ways that surpassed my highest expectations.

An old lesson had been relearned. From the lowest point that had happened in the fall of 2004 with Michael's DUI, through to Mom's passing, I rediscovered that it wasn't in my nature to stay down for too long. Not taking a moment to look back, I was off and running—on to the next amazing, incredible, fantastic adventures, with brand-new experiences on the horizon, including but not limited to: becoming the principal of my own schoolhouse—and a grandmother!

M ichael was always very thoughtful about turning down the volume on his car radio whenever he had rap or hip-hop playing and he knew I'd be riding in his car. When I heard some of the explicit language, he explained, "It's not the lyrics that I really like, it's the beat."

Actually, I liked the beat too. Between 2005 and 2008, that crazy beat created the sound track of our lives—sped up even more after Dr. Joe A. Hairston presented great news to me at Baltimore

County's Award of Excellence Celebration, where I was a featured speaker. As I sat down next to him in the large banquet hall, he told me he was appointing me the new principal of Windsor Mill School. This time, unlike a year earlier, I could answer whole-heartedly, "Thank you, sir. It would be an honor to serve. When do I start?"

He smiled and said, "Immediately."

Thirty-one years in education, almost to the day, and I had landed my dream job—not only being the principal of my own schoolhouse but helping to envision and build it from the ground up.

Dr. Joe, or Doc, as administrators also call him, could have given the position to other more senior, more experienced middle school principals. I was more or less going to be a first-time principal, even though I certainly had the administrative background and had developed award-winning programs that prepared me for the challenges ahead. Maybe it was my idealism and outside-the-box thinking that convinced him to take a chance on me. In any event, I didn't want to let him down. Most of all, I didn't want to let down the six hundred plus students whose school my team and I were going to build. In order to reduce enrollment in thirty-two over-crowded area schools, we were given the resources to open up a brand-new schoolhouse that I was going to oversee—with a most ambitious, strategic platform. It would open by the fall of 2006, a daunting goal that was placed up on the board for all of us. Our vision was not only to open the doors to the new building within a year, but more important to know that when we walked through them, we would do so with high expectations for all students for continuous improvement that would lead to increased academic success.

As I faced myriad tasks I'd never attempted before, one of my best assets was that I was never too proud to call a colleague and ask for help. And I wanted things done a certain way. When we first turned in specs for the unusual, colorful school furnishings I thought were important to creating a lively environment for learning, I promised I would cut costs on less relevant items. And I did. My attitude, however, was that the students ought to have the best, and anyone who suggested they didn't deserve to feel pride in their schoolhouse would not enjoy the conversation they would have with me.

The ribbon-cutting day in October 2006 was as close to giving birth as I had ever come without literally delivering a baby into the world. It was one of the highest-rated DP moments I could recall, and as with childbirth, the labor pains made the moment of realization all the more sweet. With my team and my family, I could stand at the groundbreaking and say, "Look what we did!"

One of my extravagances was the megaphone-shaped conference table designed to fit the shape of the administrative conference room—which I think of as my classroom or TLZ (teaching and learning zone) for my leadership team members and whoever else enters. Whether I'm meeting with students, teachers, parents, or with visiting VIPs, the table symbolizes the importance of our work together, as important in my opinion as what happens in administrative conference rooms at corporate headquarters, in university settings, or in halls of justice and government. The table also allows me to look at my staff fanned out on each side of the table during meetings at the same time that I keep an eye on the schoolhouse by checking the mirror above the table that reflects the office hallway leading to the campus behind me.

The first time I entered our atrium, I knew what needed to be in its center: a masterpiece, a large work of art that would inspire the students who came through there every day. I asked the Baltimore County Public School art office, and they identified an art teacher who might be able to assist, who in turn found high school students looking for a senior art project. In the process, a magnificent sculpture was designed and built and placed high on a platform in the atrium. It portrays an African American teacher, holding a book, with three children at his feet.

In my mind, the three children represent the diversity of our students, their learning styles, and the need for creativity on the part of all of us as educators to help them connect what they are learning to their lives and their world. We also have to be creative when students aren't where they should be educationally and when, for whatever reasons, they haven't been interacting with the world around them.

We had a situation early on when a teacher was reading directions and wanted to make sure all the students had the correct booklet, which he described by saying, "It has a picture of a seagull on the front."

A student happened to hold up the booklet and pointed to the bird on the front, asking if it was a seagull. The teacher was surprised by that question, having assumed that all the students knew what a seagull was. Rather than dwell on this lack of knowledge, I suggested we look for ways to open up students to the world around us, to arrange field trips to parks, museums, and concerts. For those teachers who aren't thinking along those lines, who need assistance, my role as principal is to use the resources that Baltimore County offers through its mentoring system. This is a visionary program that pairs teachers with teachers or administrators as mentors and mentees to make sure educators have the support and guidance to grow professionally.

And when I see creativity, innovation, and passion in the classroom, it's my job to reward it—both with students and with their teachers. And it's thrilling to be part of the growth.

An essential ingredient in that growth, I believe, is the feeling of being welcomed into your schoolhouse daily. The seasons, as always, provide the opportunity to decorate creatively, which I do after hours so I don't take a minute away from time that belongs to the students. Time spent adding to the warmth, comfort, and inviting atmosphere of our physical space, and that also honors the diversity of the students and celebrates their lives, is never "work" to me.

And where there are decorations, there really ought to be treats for teachers, parents, and students, like the hot chocolate and marshmallows served in my administrative conference room or available in the staff workroom/lounge in the Cocomotion machine, or some of my holiday season favorites that I keep stocked:

> Old-fashioned peppermint sticks, saltwater taffy, and ribbon candy (red and green)—all classics! We all love rock candy (crystallized sugar) on sticks and those raspberry sweets that are hard candies filled with fruit syrup, and anything chocolate wrapped in holiday gold.

Not to belabor the point, but I really do believe you accomplish much more with sugar, patience, love, and firmness than you ever do with vinegar. And that's a schoolhouse rule, just as everyone knows my door is open, during holidays and anytime, to students, teachers, staff, and parents alike. Not many of my working parents have time to come in, but those who do usually have sincere questions and a genuine interest in helping their children become more successful at school. Not that I have all the right answers. What I have is love, a willingness to offer support and guidance, and the hope that I can help in some way. And my approach, as always, is to be collaborative and to form a partnership. It's really not that difficult to do, provided there is a safe space where parents can air their concerns.

As a facilitator, I had a memorable experience at a school I was overseeing when a child's parents came to school to say they were confused by a teacher's comments that their daughter was unteachable. We sat in private as they repeated the educators' jargon that they'd heard and they showed me the grades and test scores they'd been sent.

The mother said, "I don't understand what they're saying."

I was so impressed that she had the confidence in me to express herself. She wasn't going to say it in front of these teachers and be embarrassed or feel ashamed.

We went over the grades and I explained them. Afterwards, the mother and father had a deeper understanding of what was being said because of the time taken to educate them about the test scores. The parents were then able to leave the school with more knowledge about their child and how to help her.

A running theme for me continued: the precious value of time. Those fifteen to thirty minutes invested in meaningful collaboration can buy a lifetime of growth. Another recent instance was a case in point. One of my students at Windsor Mill brought holiday cards to school that her mother, a single parent, had purchased to distribute to the students in the various grades. Her mother had helped her address them. I knew the expense and the effort that had been involved, and so when our teachers resisted taking the time for her to hand them out, I insisted that we make it happen.

After a teacher and I went to the cafetorium and helped organize the occasion, the student was proud to hand-deliver each card, and every recipient was just as happy to be remembered. Observers might have said that the latter portion of that lunch shift was a little chaotic, but I would call it "structured chaos." For days afterwards, I had to hold back the tears as I recalled the happy expressions on their faces. My students always notice when I forget to wear waterproof mascara!

One thing I asked for when I was appointed principal of Windsor Mill was that I would be able to travel to key competitions once Michael geared up again for the next Olympics. It turned out that Michael was barely settled in at the University of Michigan before he was back on the road testing the new strategies he and his mad scientist Bob Bowman were formulating.

One of the first meets I was determined to attend was in Austin. It was the day after a baby shower for Whitney, who was expecting her first child. During the shower Whitney disappeared on me and

I found her upstairs. When she explained that she wasn't feeling well, I decided to get her home and into bed. In the morning I left for Austin and told her to take it easy and keep her legs up. I'd be back in no time. At the meet, I got a call from Bob that Whitney was not feeling any better and that it might be time to go to the hospital.

"Let me talk to Whitney," I said. When she came on the phone, I lowered my voice but told her emphatically, "Whitney, I'm not coming home until tomorrow; you can't have this baby yet! I have to be there." I reminded her that my first baby, Hilary, took forever to arrive, so there was no hurry. "Just relax. Stay on the couch, keep your legs up, and sit tight. I'll call you later."

Michael swam magnificently, and afterward we went to a steakhouse, which he loves to do wherever he is. As we were finishing up dinner, we received the call that Whitney was at the hospital. Obviously I had to find a flight home. Michael decided he had to go too—to the consternation of Bob Bowman, who had an extremely demanding training regimen for him. Michael would need every day in the pool to pull off the impossible in Beijing. But we prevailed, not surprisingly, at least in flying into Baltimore and rushing to the hospital, where we met Hilary and dashed into Whitney's birthing room.

We were all there just in time to be on hand when our newest family member—Whitney's and Bob's baby girl Taylor—arrived in the world. Everyone immediately debated each other about who she most resembled, her mother or her father, even her aunt or uncle. Meanwhile, all I could see was Taylor, her very own person, ready to steal our hearts and to embrace her very own moments as the adventure of her life began to unfold.

By 2007 Taylor was talking up a storm, the most curious, active, loving little girl on the planet. My school was thriving. Test scores were turning around slightly. High fives for everyone. I couldn't have been any happier. It was impossible. Then we learned that Whitney and Bob were expecting again. I was even happier: my grandson Conner was on his way! Could anything dampen all this joy? Nothing.

That is, except for those things that tend to happen unexpectedly, throwing best-laid plans into disarray, requiring us to rehabilitate, reconfigure, and imagine brand-new possibilities. And, yes, there are always going to be some weeks when I need to be reminded that I'm only fine on Mondays.

We had a crazy week along those lines somewhere in the middle of 2007 when Michael had to have surgery on his hand, following a freak accident in which he banged it while getting out of his car. It has been pointed out by others that Michael's unique physiology is perfectly designed for moving through a pool in record time. His wingspan of six feet, seven inches exceeds his height (six four). He has a long torso and shorter lower frame; plus he's double-jointed, with feet like flippers and large paddlelike hands to "hold" the water. It is amazing to see Bowman conducting and Michael continually working to master the music, while maintaining his grace and seeming effortlessness while swimming. So when anything apparently minor happens—like banging his wrist—everyone worries that it could throw off that very fine tuning.

Bowman decided to go ahead and recommend that Michael have surgery to repair the wrist that had been giving him problems. Beijing was a little more than a year away and the World Championships in Melbourne were coming up. During a week when I had way too much on my plate, I went ahead and flew to Michigan to be there with him when he went to the hospital for surgery.

During the operation, Bob commented on how exhausted I appeared to be from the demands of my schedule. As he often did, Bob told me to relax, then he went to check on how the surgery was progressing and returned with a positive report. Some time passed, the operation went smoothly, and Michael woke up intent on leaving the hospital as soon as possible.

When he was moved into his own room, I went to see him with Bob, who explained that he couldn't just walk out of the hospital.

"Why not?"

Bob shot me a look. Then he explained that this was normal procedure, that at the least, you had to be at a resting heart rate, otherwise the doctors wouldn't release you.

Michael nodded and said, "I can do that."

Bob nodded in response, saying, "All right."

What was happening? Had they just decided Michael was going to lower his heart rate at will, with Bob monitoring the effort?

Sure enough, Michael leaned back and closed his eyes as he inhaled as much oxygen as he might use to swim the length of a pool underwater, and then he slowly exhaled. Bob watched him with laserlike focus, as though sending him nonverbal instructions about how to calibrate the inner movement of heart, lungs, blood, and brain control.

It was amazing to watch the two of them. After what seemed to be a matter of a few minutes, Michael's heart rate came down to normal levels.

The doctors came in and were rather startled but happily gave Michael his walking papers. In the months to come, in Melbourne for the World Championships and in Omaha the next year for Olympic trials—where Michael had overall spectacular showings— I'd often think back to that day in the hospital.

At fifteen years old, Michael declared that he wanted to change the sport of swimming, to elevate it in the eyes of fans all over the world, starting in his own backyard and across the United States. He was now twenty-two years old, almost twenty-three, and the global excitement to tune into the competition starting in Melbourne, a so-called off year for swimming, had grown exponentially from earlier World Championships I had attended. It all went back to that statement of intention—the "I can do that" of whatever it was, whether it was lowering his heart rate at will or changing the sport of swimming.

As for Beijing, anticipation was already building, and I was happy I could go to Australia to see how Michael's daunting platform was coming along. I hadn't intended to tell my students I'd be gone, but after I arrived in Melbourne, my indispensable, very wise administrative secretary, Edwina, called to suggest that I let them know after all. She told me the students were worried about my not being at school. Was I sick? Had I been fired? Had I deserted them?

My solution was to do my usual morning announcements using my cell phone. Edwina arranged for me to call in and had the line connected to the PA the next morning so the students heard me greet them as I usually did by saying, "Good morning, this is your principal." Then I added the unusual part, "I'm live here in Melbourne, Australia," and I went on to describe what I was doing there and how some of the events were going. At the end of announcements, I concluded, "For those of you who decided to come to school today in your jeans, just because I'm not at the schoolhouse doesn't mean you can break the rules. Dress code is still enforced." Most of the children knew I was joking, but others were mystified that I could see them all the way from Melbourne.

While I was in Australia, it was evident that there was a growing enthusiasm in general in the swim world. The pattern continued when the 2008 Olympic trials in Omaha rolled around. Astonishingly, it wound up being the most attended, most watched swimming competition ever held on U.S. soil. Thanks in no small measure to the added prime-time coverage from NBC Sports, where our dear friend and hero, Dick Ebersol, was at the helm, the changes in public perception about swimming and swimmers were undeniable!

When the platform for Beijing was finalized, a few people in the news media did the math. They noted that in order for Michael to go eight for eight and win every race that he'd qualified to swim—thus breaking the Mark Spitz record by winning eight gold medals in one Olympics—he'd have to compete in seventeen races including prelims and semis. Swimming seventeen races was unthinkable, let alone winning eight Olympic finals out of that count.

No one could predict whether he *would* do that. No one. But if anyone had asked me whether he *could*, I would have said, "Absolutely."

~~~~~

TWELVE

And the Rest Is History

On August 8, 2008, a date that marked the official start of the Olympic Games in Beijing and that was also believed to be auspicious—the number eight, according to Chinese numerology, represents great fortune—I beheld the fantastic spectacle of opening ceremonies. For the time being, I wasn't thinking about Michael's events coming up in two days or even how the magic number eight was relevant to him.

That night my thoughts were focused on what an honor it was to be a witness to history as China opened its doors to the world on a grander scale than had ever been mounted in any public arena and in a way that removed old barriers between nations. If the Olympic

Games could do that, I wondered, why couldn't a movement be fostered to further promote goodwill and peace through sports? In the past, I might have rejected such a sweeping vision as unrealistic. But the new mantra for everyone on Team Phelps was "Anything is possible."

That had been Michael's response every time he was asked to comment on the scope, some said impossibility, of what he was attempting to do. The phrase was all I needed in order to remain fairly relaxed until the moment of truth arrived on August 10, when Hilary, Whitney, and I went to find our seats in the Water Cube.

Fittingly, the designers of the Cube had outdone themselves, creating a modernistic cathedral to swimming with a geometric-paneled sky dome that, from the outside, gave the appearance of a sparkling cluster of aquamarine jewels dancing in the sun. Inside the Water Cube, the rays of light refracted through the dome to create the look of beautiful water bubbles and a feeling of weightlessness.

Even though it was meant to inspire a feeling of serenity, that's not what I was feeling as we waited to watch the finals of the 400-meter individual medley. And by now I couldn't get the number eight out of my thoughts.

For starters, I couldn't believe what a difference eight years had made! As millions around the world tuned in to watch how Michael would begin his pursuit of eight possible gold medals, it seemed to me that we had traveled many lifetimes to arrive at this moment. And yet everything felt as if it had taken place in the matter of a few blinks of the eye. The images made me smile to recall: the memory of a hopeful Michael at age fifteen in 2000, doing his best to find composure for his debut on the Olympic stage in Sydney; then in Athens 2004 as a phenomenally confident yet still developing nineteen-year-old; and then in the months and weeks of 2008 as he came into his own, a young man of twenty-three years, ready at last to take the world by storm as never before.

Indeed, as everyone continued to observe, for Michael to accomplish what he was attempting in Beijing was going to take a perfect storm. It would depend not only on his own performance, but also on those of his relay teammates and, for that matter, everyone on the U.S. team, along with those variables and unknowns that no one can control: health concerns like catching a bug, false-starting, illegal touch on the wall, or "wardrobe malfunctions" like leaky goggles and other things of that nature.

Then again, the whole concept of perfection, I knew by now, was not really the way life or sports should be approached. Or at least that's what I'd come to believe. Perfection isn't what gives us the gold of experience. Rather, as I had learned from some of my best teachers, it's living the greatness of the moment, seizing it, and making of it something that's beyond perfect, something lasting. It's taking everything that's come before, the lessons, the intricately plotted game plans, the discoveries, the painful passages, the mistakes, the disappointments, the ordinary and normal times, long lonely hours spent plowing the fields of practice in the pool, then releasing all of it into the mists of the past, and then just taking the dive!

True, I had to remind myself that it would be less heart-pumping and nail-biting if I could simply sit there for the next seven days and watch all eight finals, knowing everything would be perfect. But who wanted that? Not even me! All I could do, as the mom on Team

Phelps, was to be a witness, along with everyone else, to see what was going to happen in those eight moments coming right up.

So, you may wonder, was I relaxed, sitting there waiting for the first event? Not for a second! And neither were Hilary and Whitney. I was so grateful to have my daughters on either side of me, each holding one of my hands. They too had blossomed into the most amazing young women over the span of eight years. Again, it seemed as if it was yesterday that we were gathering around to hug Hilary after commencement ceremonies in the spring of 2000, when she proudly earned her bachelor's degree from the University of Richmond. Four years later, in Athens, she was already embarking on a thrilling journey with the important work that she had taken on in our nation's capital in the area of advocacy on behalf of those less fortunate. With her heart of gold and gifts for diplomacy, Hilary had become so indispensable on the work front that taking the time off to travel to Beijing wasn't all that easy to arrange. Not that she would have missed this for anything!

Whitney's eight-year journey had been no less transformational and exciting. From the decision she made at age twenty to withdraw from competition during Olympic trials in 2000 to focus on healing, she had done it her way—finding other outlets like yoga and Pilates that helped her regain strength and move past her injuries, and opening up to new possibilities both professionally and personally. The growth she had sought was evident four years later in Athens, when I remembered thinking how remarkable she was, at age twenty-four, to have the maturity, clarity, and honesty that were part of who she was. Here she was now, twenty-eight years old, happily married, the mother of two, and, not surprisingly, having managed to organize every detail for Bob's parents to hold down the fort so that she and Bob could travel to Beijing.

After Whitney's wedding, typically determined not to let anything negative detract from her happiness and sincerely excited about the next leg of my professional journey, she wrote me a short note that I will always treasure:

> *This year has been filled with a lot of surprises. I want to thank you for being there, no matter what. The wedding was amazing and you continue to shock me with your ability to get things done.*
>
> *This coming school year is going to be amazing. You are going to be a remarkable principal. I love you very much.*

With Hilary living in Washington, D.C., and my favorite son/ only son globe-trotting most of the time—otherwise known as "Where in the world is Michael Phelps?"—I was especially happy to have Whitney and her family living close by in the Baltimore area.

It was fun for me to play a role on her family team too, as the grandmother. Instead of calling me Gran as we had my mother (which most likely will occur sooner or later), Taylor referred to me simply as G—which I loved! Before long, when Conner started speaking, he would call me G as well.

Fun is serious business. Since I consider all my children to be my greatest teachers, and that includes my three kids, my two grandchildren, my students, and every child I've ever met, I had to give credit to Michael for reminding me that having fun is as important a part of a mother's job as making sure dinner is on the table on time.

My favorite life lesson learned from Michael came a few years earlier when the two of us were invited to share in a keynote at a gala that would include several dignitaries and elected officials. Every time I wanted him to go over the notes about what we were supposed to say—which had been prepared very thoughtfully—Michael said we should do it later. Finally we were on the way to the event, and I handed the pages to him. He looked at them for no more than a minute, said, "Okay, great," and handed the pages back.

"Maybe we should run through them before we go up there?"

"Okay, Mom, you can if you want to, but I am fine."

At the event, whenever I went to find him to rehearse quickly, he was in the midst of conversation, so I more or less gave up, figuring whatever happened, he would make the most of it. Then again, I wasn't quite prepared for the way he mastered the moment, rising to the occasion amazingly.

When we were announced, he was brought up first, and as if he had been doing this all his life, he dove in, just like he does when he swims, went up to the podium, put his hands on either side of the lectern, and leaned toward the crowd, speaking entirely from his heart and directly to every person in the audience.

I thought to myself, *Oh, Debbie, ye of little faith.* It was a lesson about trust. Not just about trust that Michael knew his own capacities but also about trusting myself and my own.

What a gift that was and will always be.

And now I was going to trust that whatever happened from here on out, he knew his own capacities better than any of us.

The buzzer sounded and we were off! Without keeping you in suspense one instant longer, I am happy to report that in the hunt for eight gold medals, there were moments of perfection but some close calls that made for the most unforgettable highlights ever.

That day, Michael swam the 400-meter IM in world-record time, winning gold and breaking the Olympic record he had set in the preliminaries. The eyebrow raiser in this event came during the 100 meters of the breaststroke—the stroke that he and Bob Bowman had been focused on improving. Even I leaned forward in mild surprise as I watched his mastery. Could a better start have been scripted? I don't think so! All around us were hands extended with thumbs up, hugs, cheers, and congratulations.

Sparks flew the next day in the 4×100-meter freestyle relay in which our team—Michael Phelps, Garrett Weber-Gale, Cullen Jones, and Jason Lezak, swimming in that order—had been more or less insulted by a couple of the French swimmers. Needless to say, this incident demanded even more mental fortitude on the part of the U.S. swimmers. Meanwhile, I was well aware that the pressure put on Michael's teammates was not insignificant. No one wanted to feel they'd let him down or stood in the way of his eight golds; the atmosphere behind the scenes was such that everyone kept their distance, knowing he had to stay in peak performance zone most of the time. To my knowledge, no one even discussed his goal with him or talked about it either, although it was definitely a subtext. Yet when it came time to line up for the event, everyone understood that the outcome would be determined by everyone on the team. This race was no exception, especially in the anchor leg when Jason Lezak swam miraculously from behind to overtake the French team's Alain Bernard and then rocketed to a gold-winning finish—by eight hundredths of a second, allowing the team to set a

world's record. Watching Michael and the rest of his team scream-
ing as Jason covered that much ground that quickly was a sight and
a sound never to be forgotten. The trust continued.

On August twelfth came the third race—the 200-meter freestyle—
which was 1:42:96 of Olympic brilliance. This was one of those times
when the impossible suddenly became possible. Michael attained a
speed that was almost superhuman, while making it look like effortless! Everything clicked, all the components, creating a fluidity in
this stroke with a tempo and flow that was breathtaking. For me, it
was especially validating that the 200-meter freestyle was the Olympic terrain of Ian Thorpe, the same event in which Michael had won
the bronze medal in Athens when the foreign journalist had said to
me, "Tonight the world has left your son," and I had insisted that he
was wrong. Here in Beijing, after this race, a gold medal, and a world
record, if there were any naysayers remaining, they weren't saying
much. As for those who had believed all along, it was still an arrest-
ing experience. Even Bob Bowman, not one to be overly effusive,
said, "That was pretty damn good."

Michael was now in a class of only five other athletes to have
won nine career gold medals, among them Mark Spitz and Carl
Lewis.

The next day, because of how the schedule had fallen for Michael's daunting platform, there were two finals he had to swim that
same day—the 200-meter butterfly and then the 4×200-meter freestyle relay.

The 200 fly, of course, was one of the few races where we had a
fairly strong sense that he would do well. This was, after all, his signature event. Everything went magnificently until the last 100 meters,

when Whitney noticed that Michael's stroke was tightening up. My stomach clenched. I forgot to breathe. He touched first, thankfully, winning gold, setting a new world record and moving into a class of his own as the only Olympian to have attained ten gold medals, but I was shocked to see him whip off his goggles and his swim cap the second the race was over. The last time he had done something like that, he and I had needed to have a talk about it. Well, that was immature. What on earth was going on?

Then, as we met up with fellow swim family spectators in the lobby area, we learned that his goggles had filled up with water and he had basically been swimming blind, from memory and by stroke count. All those hours of training and counting, rehearsing his races mentally and visualizing them down to the one hundredth of a second had brought him home to victory. Wow. Talk about trust with a capital T!

Now I could understand why he threw off his goggles and cap.

There was not much time to dwell on that mishap because clearly he had overcome an obstacle and was moving on—immediately. And wouldn't you know that on the same day he had only an hour between races; the 4×200-meter freestyle relay would pit the U.S. team against a powerful field that included Russia and Australia. Whitney and Hilary started to express their concern that Michael had to be feeling exhausted. But meanwhile I had started to notice that the greater his output, the more energy he had. And lo and behold, he swam his leadoff leg and smoked it, followed by fantastic performances from Ryan Lochte, Ricky Berens, and Peter Vanderkaay to keep the magic going. Another gold, another world record!

What was keeping Michael pumped by now was the count—five

down, three to go. Somehow he knew his own capacities. All we could do was trust.

Two days later the 200-meter individual medley was an occasion for me not to breathe. It was magnificent, like being in the presence of a symphony orchestra in which Michael played every instrument like a virtuoso, performing music composed by Bob Bowman. I knew the work that had gone into the preparation, but Michael truly made swimming every stroke look like pure joy, as if he was having the time of his life. This was his sixth gold and another world record.

The seventh race, the 100-meter butterfly the following day, summed up the entire experience. It was a showstopper and a cliff-hanger, better than a Triple Crown, that had us all on our feet for the entire 50.58 seconds when Michael and Milorad Čavić of the Serbian delegation battled it out for every one thousandth of a second. Coming in to the wall, Čavić, I thought, appeared to be closing. It was so tense, I couldn't watch but instead turned to the scoreboard, as I had eight years earlier at the Olympic trials. The screams all around us told me that in one last superhuman effort Michael reached and, miraculously, as I saw the scoreboard put him in first place, he touched first.

We were jumping up and down, hugging strangers, crying in disbelief. I said, "Thank God he has long fingers!"

Hilary said, "No, that was Gran behind him pushing him to the wall."

Ian Crocker, who came in fourth, said something along those lines to remind Michael how he had out-touched him in Athens in this event: "You must have a guardian angel looking over you."

We talked about it later and agreed that, without a doubt, Gran would have wanted to be on hand to see her grandson match Mark Spitz's total of seven gold medals in one Olympics.

This is how Whitney described the event in her posting on a swimblog:

I cannot find the words to describe today's swim. Sitting in the stands watching Michael go from 7th, at the 50 meter mark, to 1st was an out-of-body experience. As Michael came to the wall the entire natatorium fell silent. Everyone was unsure what the outcome had been. As I glanced up at the clock I went crazy. Michael had won the event by 1 one-hundredth of a second. I could not believe it.

At the finish Michael decided to take one final stroke and touched first by a fingernail. Thank goodness for long fingers! Mom was not able to watch the entire race and melted into her seat after finding out the results. Hilary and I jumped up and down and received congratulations from the surrounding fans. Michael was ecstatic and pumped his fists in the air and pounded the water. I was so unbelievably proud of him.

After the meet was over we were able to go down on deck and see him. My mom, Hilary, and I were so excited to see him. When we got there he was doing an interview with Mark Spitz and NBC. We were not able to speak to him one on one, but we were able to hug him. His hug was so tight and it was nice to have that moment with him. Before we left he reached into his warmup jacket and handed his GOLD medal to us. It was so beautiful and I felt honored to hold it.

The program that he has taken on during the Games has been

remarkable. He has stood up at each race and given it his all. Looking into his eyes I can tell that he is exhausted, but he has one more race left. Tomorrow morning is the 4 x 100 Individual Medley Relay and this race will too be a challenge. He has to leave everything he has in the pool and I am confident that this relay team will do a remarkable job.

This whole journey has been an amazing ride and I am so glad that I have been a part of it. I have truly enjoyed watching Michael take on the world and make history. We are leaving on Monday and I am excited to get home and see my kids. It is going to be hard to go back to reality, but I am looking forward to holding and kissing my kids.

Thank you everyone for supporting Michael and our family. The kind words and well wishes have been greatly appreciated. I am going to wrap up for the night and try to get some sleep before the last swim race of the Olympics. See you when we get home!

Does it get any better? Yes, it does!

It was at this point that I heard a new adjective had been coined to describe the accomplishment of impossible feats. What formerly had been referred to as Herculean was now being called Phelpsian.

Mark Spitz called Michael the greatest swimmer of all time and the greatest Olympian of all time, maybe even the greatest athlete of all time. When I heard that, needless to say, I had a DP moment, and I think Gran must have been very pleased as well.

Ian Thorpe, who had publicly expressed his skepticism about Michael's ability to pull off what would be henceforth referred to as

Phelpsian, later explained that he never meant to say it couldn't be done, only that he didn't think it would be done, due to obstacles that could have gotten in the way.

He was sitting not too far in front of me in the stands. Whatever he was feeling on the inside, Ian was cordial and gracious in his congratulations. Maybe he felt proud that he had provided some of the motivation for Michael to follow in his wake.

The last race, the 4×100-meter medley relay, had the U.S. team showing its prowess and its best—a magnificent way to finish on a high note. I felt nothing but pride watching Aaron Peirsol in the backstroke, Brendan Hansen swimming the breaststroke, then Michael swimming the butterfly, and the closer, Jason Lezak, bring it all home with the freestyle. I learned later that just in case there were any records left to break, Michael managed to swim the fastest butterfly split in the history of the event with this race. An eighth gold and an eighth world record. Perfect.

Eight for eight.

No matter how many times Michael stood on the podium while the national anthem played, we all cried. He was so happy that his success could reflect positively on our country, and I know it was his honor to hear this directly from President George W. Bush and First Lady Laura Bush. They were in the Water Cube to cheer during his first swim of the competition and would later honor Michael and fellow Olympians with an invitation to the White House.

Of the many admirable traits I hold dear about my son, I am always touched by his generosity and the kindness of his heart. He really does like to share his success with others and pay tribute to everyone on his team. Michael also likes to raise the bar for himself, and he is never one to be satisfied with having climbed a mountain or two; he needs an entire mountain range to conquer.

Toward that end he and Bob Bowman already had the new platform in the works. In fact, Michael wasn't at the closing ceremony in Beijing because he had flown on to London, paving the way for 2012. Aside from the training that would soon begin for that, the other undertaking was the work Michael and Bob had recently begun after purchasing the Meadowbrook facility. Their vision was to build a sports multiplex (complete with pool, gym, and ice-skating rink) that would house both the world-class swim school already in place and be the home base for further efforts to promote the sport of swimming. With further plans to possibly build or develop another facility, the two foresaw growing NBAC's membership to as many as four hundred, double the current membership.

Having won the million dollars from Speedo for breaking the Mark Spitz record, Michael promptly contributed all of it to the work of the Michael Phelps Foundation, which will fund a range of educational and public outreach projects connected to promoting swimming for health, fitness, and enjoyment, teaching water safety and drowning prevention, and inspiring the next generation of Olympic hopefuls.

As for me, besides having to hurry back to Windsor Mill to prepare for school to open, I had a few new items on my plate. I'll let Hilary Phelps give you a flavor as she did in her swimblog posting as the games came to an end:

So, it's back to reality and back to work. It really seems like just yesterday we were sitting in the Water Cube in Beijing watching

Michael make history. While getting back to "normal life" is tough, it's also been good, because it's helped me to realize just how amazing Michael's accomplishment was, and just how great of a time we had in China.

We boarded the plane in China on Monday and headed back to the States. My mom was recognized on the plane, which was surreal. But, little did I know, that it was just the beginning! On Tuesday, my mom and I headed to NYC for some media. My mom was named Johnson's Baby Mom of the Games, which is such an honor and really fitting, as she is a terrific mom!

We boarded another plane on Tuesday and headed to the Big Apple. Upon landing, we were taken to an apartment where my mom filmed a commercial that will air during Closing Ceremonies. (Make sure you tune in to Closing Ceremonies, because it's a GREAT one!) We were able to get some sleep Tuesday night and were up at 4:30 a.m. on Wednesday to start the day. We went to *Good Morning America*, *Fox & Friends*, and *Extra*. There were interviews with the *New York Post*, *In Touch*, *Wall Street Journal* and *iVillage*, just to name a few. But the most interesting thing that happened was that my mom was recognized EVERYWHERE we went! She was stopped on the street by a police officer, who told her that he had never tuned in to the Olympics but did this year because of all of the excitement. People asked for her autograph and were telling her just how proud they were of Michael and his accomplishments, and also how proud they were of her.

From the age of 15, Michael said that he wanted to elevate the sport of swimming. From what I saw in NYC, he has—a billboard in Times Square, talks of a movie, and the feeling of camaraderie that spread during these Olympic Games. It's truly amazing and only now starting to sink in.

Adventures for Team Phelps are continuing to unfold, even as I write. But this should be as good a place as any to return to where I started early on, as you may recall, when I asserted that even though life didn't turn out the way I thought it was meant to happen, it really has turned out to be better than anything I could have ever imagined. And I wouldn't have changed any of it—not a single thing.

It's been somewhat challenging lately to process all the exciting events that are occurring and that feel as if they're moving past us more swiftly than ever. That was why when I was asked recently what my favorite 2008 DP moment was, what came to mind was a night when Michael received an honor at a black-tie affair and afterwards he, Whitney, Hilary, and I decided we should go grab a bite to eat. A competition ensued for who knew the best after-hours place to go. Finally we compromised and settled on take-out Chinese food and went back to Michael's new place in Baltimore. It wasn't furnished yet but we were able to arrange some of the furniture that had just been shipped down from his brownstone in Michigan so that we could sit in the dining room at a table with a few chairs and a bench. After he went upstairs to find some sweatshirts for us to put on over our formal evening attire, we gathered happily at the table and ate our food out of the cartons.

We weren't pressed for time or rushing off, or wondering where in the world was Michael Phelps. It seemed that it had been a long time since the four of us, just a normal family, could spend quality time with one another.

I was smiling, thinking of the memory boxes I had started making for Christmas presents; I always love a present made by hand with love, as much as I love to give them. Hilary had pointed out some creative memory box ideas, and I was adding them to my own. I am happy to share them with you to perhaps inspire your own collection of memories and moments for your loved ones:

Covered boxes—like the leather-covered suitcase style I used for Michael, the tapestry fabric for Whitney, and the decorative burlap with pewter handles for Hilary. Memories included report cards, teacher notes, grade-level class photos, certificates of accomplishment, journal entries, notes, poems, news clippings, swim caps, birth certificates, bills from first doctor's visit, baby sonogram pictures, hospital bracelets, locks of hair, pressed flowers and leaves, souvenir postcards from places we've traveled so very far away.

In the process of collecting these items, I had done a lot of reflecting on the past and realized in the process that the best gift of all was what we were relishing that night: time together. I was in my element, a mother for all seasons, surrounded by the lights of my life, letting my tears fall freely with joy and thanks.

~~~~~~

Achievement Is Limitless

In honor of the birthday of Dr. Martin Luther King Jr. that was celebrated in 2009 during the week of the inauguration of President Barack Obama, I was thrilled to be invited to speak at a Baltimore County elementary school as part of a program called "Dreaming of Change."

I was told that I could say anything, but if possible they wanted me to touch on the theme of diversity and also to weave in thoughts about Dr. King and President Obama and, of course, Michael Phelps. On the drive there, I began to get a few ideas, but it wasn't until I was seated in the gymnasium, watching the amazing creativity and talent of the students, that I knew how to frame my thoughts. I was inspired by their two-hour program, which included dance, classical music, choral performances, songs about Dr. King and Barack Obama, and poetry recited in English and Spanish. The hope and excitement that were so prevalent in this time was certainly in the air in this room.

When it came time for me to speak, I first had to applaud all the children who were in attendance, and I invited them to help me with the best applause we could offer. They were very proud to applaud each other.

Then we applauded their parents. The joy and pride on their faces as they watched their children was infectious. "Maybe we should give the parents another round of applause," I suggested, and everyone was happy to oblige. Then we recognized the administration and teachers as well with more applause.

Seeing as they were with me so far, I told them that my part of the program was to talk about three different individuals who had three commonalities. I called my subject "three and three."

The children were very quiet, leaning toward me, waiting to see where this was going.

"The three different individuals were born at very different times. First there was an individual who was born on a date close to today, January 15, 1929, and that was Dr. Martin Luther King Jr. And this week we celebrate the eightieth anniversary of his birth."

A spontaneous cheer went up for Dr. King.

"There is another individual that I would like to talk about whose birthday is June 30, 1985, which would make him twenty-three. Um, who might that be?"

They asked for a hint.

"I do know him a little better than Dr. King. Really, I know him a lot better."

And the audience yelled, "Michael Phelps!" with much excitement and enthusiasm.

"There is a third person whose birthday is different. It's August 4, 1961, and he is forty-seven years old. Do you know who that might be?"

From the audience a few of the children asked, "A new president?"

"That's right," I continued, "and his name is?"

In unison several more students called out, "Barack Obama!"

Well, of course they were correct.

We talked about the diversity of three different individuals, born in different places in different years. One of them was African American, another was white, and the third was biracial. "One would have been eighty years old this week, the other is twenty-three, and the third is forty-seven. So what do you think they all have in common?"

In great suspense, the crowd waited for me to point out what their commonalties were. "They each had a dream, they each had vision, and they had goals they wanted to achieve."

We went through each of their stories, starting with Dr. King's dream of equality for all people and how he had a vision to work toward his dream by setting many goals. We talked about young Barack Obama, who had a dream that someday he could be president of the United States and a vision that anybody could grow up to achieve their dreams. But then, just to make sure they were with me, I asked, "And what did he need to achieve them?"

Practically every child in there called out, "Goals!"

"What about Michael Phelps? What did he need first to become the greatest Olympian in the world?"

"A dream!"

"And what did he have that allowed him to see that it was possible to do that, just like Barack Obama believed he could grow up to be president?"

"A vision!"

"And what did he set to make his vision come true?"

"Goals!"

My message to the students was also to their parents—that achievement is limitless. This message is in the mission statement that accompanies every piece of correspondence sent out from Windsor Mill Middle School. It's what I believe and what I teach—as a mother, a grandmother, a principal, and a cheerleader from a small town in western Maryland.

When I closed my portion of the program, I asked the children to close their eyes and think of their dreams. Maybe they wanted to be a great leader like Dr. Martin Luther King Jr., who would inspire others to follow their dreams. Maybe they had a vision to become president of the United States, an Olympic athlete, or a world-class musician, or a great teacher, doctor, painter, computer expert. It was all up to each of them to use their imagination—just as Michael did—and let it take them as far as they wanted to go.

Many of the adults had tears in their eyes. We were all feeling excited about the new season in our country's history. Who was to say we couldn't solve our problems if we all dared to believe that achievement is limitless for all of our children and for all of us? What a wonderful opportunity and time of possibilities!

In such an inspired state of mind, a few days later I traveled to Washington, D.C., to take part in a preinaugural event, the Children's Inaugural Ball with the Every Child Matters Education Fund at the National Historical Society. That was a day of events celebrating the contribution to children made by every president. Hilary, Whitney, and Taylor were there when I did a reading to a very bright, charming group of young children.

In the hospitality suite afterwards, I was spotted by one of the young performers, who did a double take and came over, asking, "I know you, don't I? I have seen you on TV."

Nodding my head, I said, "Maybe."

"Of course," she went on. "You have that cooking show!"

Hilary and Whitney immediately chimed in, "Cooking show? Not her." They tried to explain that I had many talents as a mother and a background in home economics, but cooking was never my thing.

But then again, you never know. As a lifelong learner, I might tackle it again one day. Or I'll leave it to the members of my immediate and extended family like my daughters, my sisters, B.J., and Bob Bowman—all of whom definitely know their way around the kitchen.

Bowman cooks like he does everything else—to perfection or not at all. Based upon that logic, he recently decided that since he didn't have enough time to devote to his racehorces, he needed to sell them. There had been a running bit between him and Michael about Bob's refusal to name any of his horses Phelps. He named one Vanderkaay after two brothers who swim for the U.S. team, so Michael couldn't understand why he didn't have a horse named for him. Bob's excuse? The horse would develop an inferiority complex because nobody could live up to the Phelps name.

Well, that had been the standing joke up until the downside of the celebrity associated with his name became woefully apparent during the 2009 Super Bowl weekend—when we lived through something along the lines of "déjà vu all over again" as Yogi Berra once said so profoundly. It was then, during the aftermath of the media deluge stirred by a British tabloid photograph of Michael taken at a college party, that I was reminded of something my son said to me in the wake of his D.U.I. when he admitted, "Right now, I want to be anybody else but Michael Phelps."

Of course, that broke my heart to hear then, as it did during this challenging time. Like any parent or family member would react when their loved one might have engaged in disappointing, un-characteristic behavior, I was, as Michael expressed to a reporter, "Not happy."

Let me quickly add, however, that as the mother for all seasons that I'm committed to being, I could not have been more proud of how Michael dealt with the onslaught, taking full responsibility for his actions, not blaming anyone but himself. Michael has not only taken his lumps, recommitting himself to the sport he loves, but has gone even further by promising never to repeat the mistakes that have let his admirers down.

The painful though essential life lesson for all of us, I think, is that if we believe that achievement is limitless and we dare to set the bar high for ourselves, it doesn't guarantee that we will win at everything or that we won't err or falter. Again, we're all human. And so, too, are our Olympians and our most revered athletes. As one of the next projects that I intend to undertake—with a note to myself not to limit my own possibilities—I'd like to do more to energize our Olympic movement not just to train our athletes to become champions, but also to give them opportunities after victory to find structure and focus in arenas other than the field of competition.

This challenging season is only one valley among more peaks to come, I know. But it has provided me with a deeper understanding of what being a champion really is. As Michael has shown me, the true test of being a champion is what you do when you've fallen or made those missteps and whether or not you give up, or are willing to dust yourself off, get up off the ground, stand tall, and then dive right back in the pool.

The gift of witnessing those efforts have resulted in more DP moments, you can be sure!

They continue to sneak up on me sometimes when I'm not expecting them at all—like on the recent gloomy, overcast Maryland day when I drove down to Frederick to attend a swim meet at Hood College. My nephew, Andrew, a freshman at Salisbury State University, walked on this past year to join the swim team and I couldn't miss this meet. This was to be my first time anywhere near a pool since Beijing. Just over six months, and so much had happened already since then. When I got out of the car and approached the swim center—a kind of bubble structure that had been placed over what was once an outdoor short-course pool—I had to admit that it was a far cry from the Water Cube. My sister Amy and her husband, David, were excited that there was a large contingency of us to cheer for Andrew: me, Hilary, Whitney, and Taylor, along with Donna, B.J., and Krista.

Honestly, I didn't expect to be so emotional. But as I entered the bubble complex, which was very warm and steamy inside, and I smelled the first waft of chlorine, I felt right at home. Watching Andrew swim, of course, brought back lots of memories. As the anchor swimming freestyle for a medley relay, he performed wonderfully, helping his team cruise to second place. Looking around at the faces of everyone seated in rows of folding chairs around the pool, I smiled just from imagining all the dreams and possibilities in the futures of their loved ones. And of course I couldn't hide my delight that Taylor, who had just started Montessori preschool, was especially eager to get in the water and swim.

But the true DP moment, when I was so grateful for waterproof mascara, was at the beginning when we all turned to the flag and the national anthem was sung. It gets me every time!

ACKNOWLEDGMENTS

Few experiences in life come close to the act of giving birth, but I am convinced that writing a book must be one of them. It simply wouldn't have been possible without the tireless efforts of Team DP, nor would it have been as fulfilling and meaningful. My deepest gratitude goes to everyone at Octagon, each of whom personifies grace under fire—especially Peter Carlisle. Thank you for your wisdom, your caring, and your steadying hand. I'm indebted as well to Laisee Rintel, Niki Sollinger, Ben Morrill, Drew Johnson, Marissa Gagnon, and Frank Zecca. Thanks to everyone there for giving me and my book the same love and positive energy that distinguishes everything Octagon does!

I want to express a very special thanks to my collaborator, Mim Eichler Rivas, a midwife on this book. From the start of our process, I knew that I'd found a kindred spirit who was able to guide me onto new turf so that the stories, tears, and laughter could flow. Even with our time constraints, it was such an enriching and fruitful experience in which we were able to maximize every minute together—whether while breaking bread or taking a ride back through the memories. Thanks for sharing your family who were part of the team too.

My appreciation also goes to Farley Chase at the Waxman Agency for your help, and to our editor, Henry Ferris, for your expert guidance, as well to everyone at William Morrow. Thank you all for your commitment to greatness.

I will never forget the contribution of those family members and friends who granted interviews and read a few drafts of the "baby" as it was progressing. Thank you Hilary Phelps, Michael Phelps, and the four Flickingers—Whitney, Bob, Taylor, and Conner. You provided the heart of the book whenever I went off course. B.J. Davisson, a fond thanks is in order for prodding my memory to recall some of our shared stories. You're my favorite brother and only brother! And Bob Bowman, aka Leonard Bernstein, your additions helped provide some of the soaring music on these pages—just a prelude for the book you will be writing next!

To ALL my family and friends too numerous to name individually, this journey wouldn't have been the same without you all cheering me on at every step of the way.

As for those members of Team DP at Windsor Mill Middle School, my colleagues, including but not limited to everyone at

Baltimore Country Public School District and the Fab Five (in whose company I'm so proud to be a fellow principal and woman), along with all the individuals throughout our extended family who I hold so dear in my heart, I don't know where to begin to say thank you or how to express my appreciation. You are all part of this book. And that includes all of my former, current, and future students, and your families. Each and every one of you is the reason for my every season. I love you and thank you ALL!